Enthusiastic Praise for
Digging Deep

"*Digging Deep* teaches the art of living creatively—from envisioning and creating the garden of your dreams to cultivating and embodying more imagination, passion, and play in your daily life. A profound and inspiring book."

—**Andrew Weil, M.D.** #1 *New York Times* best-selling author of *Spontaneous Happiness*

"Fran Sorin knows how gardening takes root in the soul. Her book abounds with inspiring stories and activities to get you into the garden and to get the most out of it. Whether you're a beginner or a lifetime gardener, you'll find much to celebrate in *Digging Deep*."

—*USA Weekend Magazine*

"From wishing and hoping to weeding and hoeing, Sorin enthusiastically guides gardeners every step of the way, helping them to learn how to make choices and sharpen skills, celebrate successes, and embrace changes from a more creative perspective."

—*The American Library Association*

"Sorin views gardening as the perfect place to begin one's creative reawakening."

—*Booklist Reviews*

"Full of inspiring stories, creative exercises, and practical gardening tips, *Digging Deep* will help you bloom along with your garden."

—**Marci Shimoff,** *New York Times* best-selling author of *Happy for No Reason*

"While *Digging Deep* focuses on gardening, readers can apply the wisdom and lessons in the book to any creative pursuit. The message? Being creative fulfills and nourishes us deep within. Mindful gardening is what Sorin wants us to practice."

—*Pacific Sun*

"In *Digging Deep*, Sorin explores the experience of gardening on a variety of levels and provides her own insights based on a lifetime of planning, digging, planting, maintaining her own garden and designing gardens for others. . . . She shares an extraordinary gift for making important points gained through a life of gardening."

—**Mark Cullen,** *Toronto Star*

"Captivating and enchanting! Fran Sorin understands that a garden should be a playground for our imaginations, and a place that is as lively, entertaining, and ever-changing as our own creative spark. A must-read for anyone who wishes to find themselves in the garden—and for everyone who didn't know they could."

—**Amy Stewart**, author of *The Drunken Botanist*

"This book has heaven's kiss of inspiration upon it! Fran Sorin is a muse, revealing how the art of gardening powerfully activates the creative force within, invigorating and unifying us in body, mind, and spirit."

—**Michael Bernard Beckwith,** author of *Life Visioning*

"*Digging Deep* strikes a deep chord about the sacred act of gardening and humankind's primal need to get our hands in the earth and connect with nature. For Fran Sorin, gardening is a playful ritual that transcends our normal consciousness—it's pure rapture and a profound tool for creating meaning and beauty. *Digging Deep* is a spiritual treasure."

—**Fr. Richard Rohr, O.F.M.**, author of *Eager to Love*

"If I were categorizing this book, I'd invent the term **garden therapy**. Though the chapters include instructions on actual plant cultivation, the reason to read *Digging Deep* is for its lessons in creativity. Your garden is a perfect place to imagine, explore, play, work, risk, share, and celebrate."

—**Carnegie Library of Pittsburgh, Staff Pick**

"Sorin sees the garden as an extension of the gardener, and *Digging Deep* is devoted to coaxing the unique statement out of the person, not the soil. As such, it is more a self-help book than gardening text."

—*San Antonio Express-News*

"Sorin gardens on two levels, both physically and metaphysically. A familiar face on television and voice on radio, the longtime broadcaster and popular motivational speaker approaches gardening like yoga. *Digging Deep* rejuvenates the mind and spirit as well as exercises muscles."

—*The Sacramento Bee*

"Gardening is good for the soul! In *Digging Deep*, Fran Sorin reveals how the act of gardening helps to cultivate the creativity and joy of your true nature."

—**Robert Holden Ph.D.**, author of *Happiness NOW!*

"Fran Sorin is a philosopher-gardener whose love for plants and people shines through every page. *Digging Deep* is a lens that gives a fresh look at the art of growing things. By connecting gardening with what is most fundamental in our own lives, she shows how it is a creative pursuit that nourishes body and soul."

—**Debra Lee Baldwin**, author of *Designing with Succulents*

"The garden is where any and all who are willing to be an apprentice to nature's mysteries can learn not just the secrets of the earth. . . but of themselves, as well. To gain this true self-knowledge, all that's required is *Digging Deep*. Thanks to Fran Sorin for reminding us of this essential spiritual instruction."

—**Guy Finley**, author of *The Secret of Letting Go*

"Anyone lucky enough to dig into this deep book will learn a great deal about opening the book of nature and experiencing creative awakening. Fran Sorin's Seven Stages of Creative Awakening can help anyone cultivate a happier, more fulfilled, and joyful life. Much wisdom and genuine delight is to be found in these pages."

—**Lama Surya Das**, author of *Awakening the Buddha Within*

"*Digging Deep* is a gardening bible for the disbeliever—a gentle and inspiring guide to the spiritual journey awaiting you in your own backyard. Sorin tells anyone who has ever attempted, abandoned, or avoided gardening exactly how and where to start. Beautiful, helpful, and wise."

—**Karen Maezen Miller**, author of *Paradise in Plain Sight*

"*Digging Deep* is a guided pathway to deepening your own creative nature through gardening. The principles and practices in this book will strengthen you as a visionary and a creator of something new that reflects your most authentic self.

—**Elizabeth Murray**, author of *Living Life in Full Bloom*

"Fran Sorin believes we are all creative and has written a book that will speak to your soul. While *Digging Deep* focuses upon gardening, you can apply the lessons and wisdom shared in this book to any creative pursuit you wish.

—**Angela Artemis**, author of *The Intuition Principle*

Digging Deep is a delight, and a must-read for anyone who thinks they aren't creative. Fran will take you through the steps of removing that stifling 'I'm not creative' voice from your mind and replacing it with encouraging words and concrete actions that will help release your inner artist."

—**Rebecca Sweet**, author of *Refresh Your Garden
Design with Color, Texture & Form*

"Returning to the garden is more than a metaphor for spiritual awakening; it is a practice for achieving it as well. Fran Sorin has been showing us how to realize the unity of God, woman, man, and nature through gardening for many years, and the New Revised Edition of *Digging Deep: Unearthing Your Creative Roots Through Gardening* is another example of her ripening wisdom."

—**Rabbi Rami Shapiro**, author of
Perennial Wisdom for the Spiritually Independent

"Fran Sorin got to the heart of creativity with *Digging Deep*. It's a reflective read giving permission to be creative in one's spirit and garden. A must read for anyone who is searching for the good in the garden. . . in nature. . . in love. . . in life."

—**Helen Yoest**, author of *Plants With Benefits*

"*Digging Deep* illustrates that we all have a creative spark and provides easy-to-use tools to nurture that spark along. Recommended for anyone who wants more than just a technical primer, but instead a guide to creating a garden that is uniquely personal."

—**Susan Morrison**, author of *Garden Up!*

"In the same fashion that *The Artist's Way* made us rethink the artist within, Fran Sorin's *Digging Deep* is a guide to slow down and consider gardening as a road to personal discovery—while we bask in the moment, day-by-day."

—**Dee Nash**, author of *The 20-30 Something Garden Guide*

"*Digging Deep* is a leisurely, sensuous, and thoughtful journey into the creation of your own garden. It's a step-by-step guide in which the unique way you see and think is as important as how you till the soil or choose a sturdy rose plant."

—**Trebbe Johnson**, author of *The World Is a Waiting Lover*

"*Digging Deep* introduces us to the act of gardening as a creative and spiritual pursuit. In this gem of a book, Fran Sorin shows how to cultivate creativity as we cultivate the earth! Her book is full of practical garden ideas as well as delightful exercises. *Digging Deep* should be on every gardener's book list."

—**Jan Johnsen**, author of *Heaven is a Garden*

"Fran Sorin has written an inspiring 'how to' gardening guide that invites you to slow down, experiment, and let your imagination and playful spirit unleash themselves. The hands-on exercises throughout the book will get you out of your head and into your heart. *Digging Deep* will enable you to not only become the artist of your garden, but of your life, as well."

—**Debra Prinzing**, author of *Slow Flowers*

"A garden is a slice of heaven, a divine and peaceful retreat from the cluttered world. In *Digging Deep*, Fran Sorin arms her readers with inspiration, insight, and ingenuity, teaching us how to create a garden ripe with serenity and significance."

—**Jessica Walliser**, author of *Attracting Beneficial Bugs to Your Garden*

" Fran Sorin has created the ideal book for the weary grown-up in you to take back to that left-behind kid. Buy it, wrap it carefully with paper and twine, and present it as both a promise and gift. You'll find that *Digging Deep* is a kind book of small doable steps, a road map, a book filled with permission and exercises that you can read and work on as you find your way back to that playful, wonder-filled part of you."

—**David Perry**, photographer, *The 50 Mile Bouquet*

"In *Digging Deep*, Fran Sorin encourages readers to transform gardening from a simple task into a sacred practice that fosters creativity and connection. Each page transmits her joyful, childlike curiosity and her infectious enthusiasm for sun, seed, and soil. Read this book, and you'll delight in the dirt like never before."

—**Cara Bradley**, author of *On The Verge: Wake Up, Show Up, and Shine*

DIGGING
Deep

DIGGING

Deep

UNEARTHING YOUR CREATIVE ROOTS
THROUGH GARDENING

FRAN SORIN

BRAIDED
WORLDS
Philadelphia

Printed in the United States of America. First Edition: Warner Books.
New Revised Edition: Braided Worlds Publishing.

For information, contact:

Braided Worlds Publishing
1810 Rittenhouse Square
Philadelphia, PA 19103
Email: info@braidedworldspublishing.com

For foreign and translation rights, contact Nigel J. Yorwerth
Email: nigel@PublishingCoaches.com

Library of Congress Control Number: 2015921016

10 9 8 7 6 5 4 3 2 1

Digging Deep: unearthing your creative roots through gardening/Fran Sorin.

ISBN: 978-0-9907919-3-5
eBook ISBN: 978-0-9907919-4-2

1. Garden essays and design 2. Creative ability—Problems, exercises, etc. 3. Self-actualization—(Psychology)—Problems, exercises, etc.

Cover Design: Nita Ybarra
Interior illustrations:
 Dover Publications
 Vintageprintable1 *(www.flickr.com/photos/vintageprintabledotcom)*
 The Graphics Fairy *(www.thegraphicsfairy.com)*

Contents

Foreword
to the New Revised Edition

Gardening in many wisdom traditions is a way of communing with the Transcendent, a portal into another world. The garden is a meeting place for the sacred and the secular, the human and the divine. It is an affirmation of life itself. Gardening civilizes us, heals us, inspires us. So, whether you tend a sprig of ivy in your office or a large plot of vegetables, let gardening be a path toward wholeness of body, mind, and spirit. Fran Sorin, in this wonderful book, shows the way.

I resonate strongly with *Digging Deep* and am honored to offer words of support. Fran's premise is personal for me: I grew up on a farm, have vegetable-gardened for years, and consider gardening as both a practical and spiritual pursuit.

Fran is keenly aware that immersion in gardening and the green world are not merely casual hobbies but are sacred ventures. She knows that human welfare and plants are intertwined, and that human life and plant life go hand in hand. Quite simply, without plants, we would die.

One of my favorite quotations is from the late humorist, Erma Bombeck, who said, "Never go to a doctor whose office plants have died." Her witticism captures how plants mirror our attitudes toward life. And it reminds me how I used to keep a variety of plants in my medical office—jade plants, Janet Craig dracaenas, ferns, and, in season, blooms cut from my garden.

We sense that we are connected with plants at a deep level. This awareness is revealed in our language. It's as if we *are* plants. We grow like "weeds" in childhood, "blossom" as we mature, and go to "seed" as we age. New ideas get "planted" in our minds, where they "germinate," "take root," "flower," or "wither." We "weed" out bad ideas, "cultivate" good will, and "reap" what we "sow." We raise "seed" money for new businesses, "farm" out projects to others, and join "grass-roots" movements. We collect "kernels" of wisdom, follow decision "trees," and "branch out" in our activities. We may go out on a "limb" and get lost in a "jungle" of detail. Someone who doesn't see the big picture is a "blooming" idiot who can't see the "forest" for the "trees." Surgeons perform "implants" and "transplants," and physicians do "stem" cell research. We "leaf" through books and turn over new "leaves" in our behaviors.

These expressions point to our "green consciousness", the fundamental psychospiritual connections we share with the plant world.

The importance of gardening and "digging deep" is written into our physiology. Evidence for what's called the "hygiene hypothesis" is abundant. Briefly, we know that children who are exposed to dirt in their formative years develop healthier, stronger immune systems when compared to children whose parents keep them squeaky clean, and they have a lower incidence of asthma, eczema, and allergies later in life.[1] Exposure to dirt in childhood promotes good health. Any type of exposure will do; romping on a sand pile or in a sand box, making mud pies, or my favorite, teaching kids to garden. It's not a hard sell to the kids: They usually adore these experiences. It's parents who can need a bit of convincing, having been taught that cleanliness is always preferred, germs are always bad, and so on.[1]

Adults benefit from exposure to dirt as well. Studies show that an individual's mood is elevated when he or she is exposed to microbes commonly found in garden soil—dirt as psychotherapy.[1]

Gardening is one of the most potent ways of opening the unconscious, allowing thoughts we usually keep suppressed to surface in our awareness. From personal experience, I call these moments "garden thoughts" or "yard thoughts" because they bubble up while doing mindless yard work as well as gardening. I've had creative thoughts erupt spontaneously more times than I can count while digging in the dirt.

Fran Sorin knows how to listen to plants. Our ancestors also knew how to listen to what plants have had to say. In ancient Greece, priestesses and priests in the sacred grove at Dodona interpreted the rustling of the oak or beech leaves to determine the correct actions to be taken. As Shakespeare says in *Macbeth,* "Stones have been known to move and trees to speak." The talent for listening endures: in some regions, it flourishes. When biologist Lyall Watson asked native herbalists on Madagascar how they knew which plants were useful for a particular illness, they responded, "Oh, it's easy. We ask the plants." By asking, they knew, for example, that the periwinkle plant was useful for "milky blood" or leukemia long before modern researchers discovered it.[2]

Gardening is a pathway into an understanding of the unity, connectedness, and "fittingness" of all things, including things green. As Black Elk, the Lakota medicine man said, "It is the story of all life that is holy...us two-leggeds sharing in it with the four-leggeds and the wings of the air and all the green things."[3]

Fran Sorin's intimate, reverential relationship with plants comes through on every page of *Digging Deep*. Her intimacy with the green world is part of a long tradition that surfaces regularly in human experience. As Charles Darwin concluded in his later years, "The more I look at plants, the higher they rise in my mind."[4]

Signs of kinship with plants are everywhere if you know how to look. While visiting New York City a few years ago, I was walking along a sidewalk in a residential area on Manhattan's East Side. I glanced mindlessly up at the facade of a lovely old brownstone and saw a carved face leering down at me from the third-floor level. The ornate stone head was crowned with leaves that spilled onto the brow and face and emerged from the mouth. I had stumbled onto the Green Man.

The Green Man is a mythic theme from pagan times that has survived in numerous images in old European churches. He is usually depicted as a face covered with leaves, and frequently has leaves coming out of his mouth. The Green Man images are remarkably varied and are frequently executed with stunning sensitivity. They are found in churches from the Gothic period all over England, France, and Germany—in carvings tucked away in corners or under lintels and pedestals, holding up figures of saints, popes, and bishops, or in stained glass. Ralph Metzner, an authority on the Green Man tradition, writes that the cathedral builders seemed to be saying, "This is the hidden root of spiritual power in nature, without which the church could not stand."[5]

The Green Man images do not call attention to themselves. They are so unobtrusive that you can walk through the churches and never see them, but once you develop an eye for them they seem to be everywhere. This was the experience of two friends of mine in

England, Stephen Wright and Jean Sayre-Adams, nurse-researchers and co-authors of the book *Sacred Space*.[6] Stephen had been unaware of the Green Man, although he has lived in England all his life. "[But] since you mentioned it," he says, "we're seeing the damned thing everywhere."

I know the feeling. One day, I was sitting in my living room reading. I happened to glance mindlessly at a heavily carved bookcase my wife and I have owned for 20 years and realized, for the very first time, that the strange, three-inch carved faces on either side of the bookcase were images of the Green Man! Leaves streamed from both sides of their faces and heads, and from their chins flowed cascades of leaves and pear-shaped fruit. I was astonished, and more than a little embarrassed, that I could live in the same house with two excellent carvings of the Green Man and not know it.

Is it any accident that many of the world's loftiest visions of creation and paradise are set in gardens such as Eden? Psychologist C. G. Jung believed that plants were links to the mind of God, however the Absolute is named. "The earthly manifestations of 'God's world' began with the realm of plants, as a kind of direct communication from it. It was as though one were peering over the shoulder of the Creator...."[7] Plants as mediators with the Divine. I am pretty sure Fran Sorin would agree.

Larry Dossey, M.D.
Author of *One Mind: How Our Individual Mind Is Part of a Greater Consciousness and Why It Matters*[8]

Endnotes

1. Larry Dossey. Dirt. In: *The Extraordinary Healing Power of Ordinary Things*. New York, NY: Random House/Harmony; 2006: 72-93.

2. Lyall Watson. *Jacobson's Organ*. New York, NY: W.W. Norton; 2000: 194.

3. Black Elk. Quoted in: *Restoring the Earth: Visionary Solutions from the Bioneers*. Kenny Ausubel, ed. Tiburon, Cal: H.J. Kramer; 1997:6.

4. Joel L. Swerdlow, and Ari D. Johnson. Living with microbes. *Wilson Quarterly*. Spring 2002; XXVI (2): 42-59.

5. Ralph Metzner. *Green Psychology*. Rochester, Vermont: Park Street Press. 1999:138-140.

6. Stephen Wright and Jean Sayre-Adams. *Sacred Space: Right Relationship and Spirituality in Healthcare*. New York, NY: Churchill Livingstone; 2000.

7. Carl G. Jung. *Memories, Dreams, Reflections*. Aniela Jaffé, ed. Richard and Clara Winston, trans. Revised edition. New York, NY: Vintage/Random House; 1965:67-68.

8. Larry Dossey. *One Mind: How Our Individual Mind Is Part of a Greater Consciousness and Why It Matters*. Carlsbad, CA: Hay House; 2103.

Foreword

I first met Fran Sorin when she was an eighteen-year-old student at The University of Chicago where I was a Professor of Psychology. She approached me one evening after I had just given a speech and told me that she wanted to work with me. Because of her unbridled enthusiasm, I took Frannie on as one of my assistants. She became one of my students and also did her psychology honors research under my direction on the subject of "Creativity in Schizophrenics." Even as a student, it was obvious to me that Frannie was not only highly intelligent and curious, but that she possessed an optimistic and creative nature that would serve her well in life.

When Fran Sorin graduated with Honors in Psychology, little did I realize that she would ultimately become a talented garden designer. None of it surprises me, although it delights me. The core of Frannie's personality has always consisted of a deep desire to understand the human condition and her own belief that all humans have the ability and need to live a creative existence. I have observed her time and again for over thirty years, risking herself both personally and professionally in order to get closer to her own creative essence.

As an international expert in the fields of hypnosis, altered states of consciousness, dream interpretation, and creativity, I always find it quite magical to see someone such as Frannie, who spends little time discussing theories but is actually experiencing an incredibly creative life. From the time she was five years old, Frannie had access to an altered state of consciousness through studying piano. It is only now, forty years later, that she is prepared to talk about the beauty of the process, using gardening as the tool and metaphor.

When Fran Sorin walks into a room, she radiates joyfulness. Her manner implies that this world is a wonderful, exciting place in which to live. I urge you to listen to what she has to say. Her thoughts and ideas are powerful and can help you approach your own life with a heightened awareness and a more celebratory nature. *Digging Deep* will surely be a groundbreaking book.

Erika Fromm, Ph.D.
Author of *Self-Hypnosis: The Chicago Paradigm,*
1910–2003

Preface
to the New Revised Edition
of *Digging Deep*

Gardening is a sacred act.

When you dig a hole in the ground and feel the soil in the palm of your hand, or as it crumbles between your fingers, you're participating in a ritual that's been taking place since the dawn of humankind.

There's a rhythm to gardening that soothes our souls and awakens our senses. It's through observing and celebrating the change of seasons that we can learn to accept our own human journey from gestation to birth, death, and beyond.

Working in the garden over time, we learn to appreciate the Japanese aesthetic, wabi-sabi. Everything is imperfect, impermanent, and incomplete. Eventually, often without even trying, we discover ourselves sinking into the wabi-sabi of life. We become less judgmental of ourselves and others and find ourselves more accepting of our own humanness.

Throughout my childhood, whenever I practiced the piano, I would have what the renowned humanistic psychologist, Abraham Maslow, called a *peak experience*. Later, as a young mother with two toddlers, gardening drew me once again into this extraordinary state of consciousness. Joseph Campbell called it *rapture*, Mihaly Csikszentmihalyi, *flow*, and Carl Rogers, *self-actualization*.

Regardless of what label is used to describe this state—be it psychological, anthropological, or spiritual—it boils down to the same thing. When we move beyond the realm of ordinary consciousness, we enter a world of sacred play where all self-consciousness is stripped away. It's an uncensored and safe place where our childlike nature is free to frolic, imagine, and create without fear of repercussions or consequences.

Discovering the magic that takes place in the garden and in life every day enables you to open to experiencing feelings of freedom and peace and engage in a playful type of creating, without worrying about the results. It's play for the sake of play.

It's also the place where we feel the most free to slip into a meditative, mindful state of being. Perhaps there are times when you go out to do some weeding or deadheading and end up becoming mesmerized by the texture of a rose petal, or a ladybug scrambling up a leaf, or the branches of a tree swaying in the autumn breeze, its leaves slowly scattering on the ground. In that frame of mind, you're totally focused on the profound beauty and magic of nature. You're fully present, simply observing and *being*, without producing anything. Although you may not actively be creating something, you're in a receptive mode of deep gratitude for the moment-by-moment creativity with which nature envelops you. As you closely observe each autumn leaf, dancing in slow motion through the air, you become exquisitely aware of its unique journey toward the earth, for no two leaves' movements are the same. Being in this zen-like state opens up your creative pores, freeing your authentic self from a censored place.

Seven Stages of Creative Awakening

When I wrote *Digging Deep* in 2004, it was a groundbreaking book. At that time, there were few gardening books, if any, that addressed gardening as a spiritual/creative/transformational process.

In the years since it was first published, *Digging Deep* has become a classic. Although I've spent the last twenty-five years guiding individuals to get their hands in the earth and use gardening as a tool for well-being and joy—through extensive writing, broadcasting, workshops, and speaking—my desire for the book was that its growth be organic, and that its ideas be embraced and shared with others. I'm grateful that this is exactly what happened. I regularly receive notices about courses being taught at botanical gardens and creativity forums based upon the book's Seven Stages of Creative Awakening. I also receive a steady stream of letters from people who share their appreciation of how *Digging Deep* has made an impact on their lives. I've heard from readers how they've made career changes, gone from being timid gardeners to confident ones, pursued creative endeavors that they had put on the back burner, and made significant changes in their relationships (for the better!). Some even tell me how they pay it forward with *Digging Deep*: Because the book has had such a profound effect on them, they buy several copies to share with friends, colleagues, and family members. The idea that this book has helped people not only connect with nature—becoming intimately acquainted with its cycles and secrets—but with their own true nature, as well, and that they want to share this experience with others, touches me deeply.

When I speak or give workshops, I'm pleasantly surprised and delighted when someone from the crowd who isn't a gardener approaches me to say how much *Digging Deep* has helped them get unstuck and discover their creativity. Although I know the Seven

Stages of Creative Awakening have the power to be used in all areas of life to unearth and connect with our creative essence, it's still wonderful to hear how the book has inspired non-gardeners to bring more elements of play into their lives, take creative risks they might not have even thought about before, or develop a connection with nature that they hadn't experienced since childhood. Consciously making changes in your life to get closer to your real self is similar to planting seeds in a garden. One small change, perhaps exploring an unfamiliar neighborhood, plants a seed that will inevitably bloom into a beautiful flower. So as you work on strengthening your creativity muscles over time, your life becomes like a garden in full bloom— rich with color, texture, movement, and *gloriosity*.

My garden, in the suburbs of Philadelphia where I worked, played, and raised my family for over twenty-five years, was deeply rooted in my soul. Yet, a few years after *Digging Deep* was published, I began to feel the rumblings of a shift taking place. My spirituality had deepened, in large part due to my gardening. I was yearning to participate in a spiritual community where I could learn about faith-based religions with other like-minded individuals. Thanks to a dear friend, and a helpful nudge from synchronicity, I enrolled at One Spirit Interfaith Seminary in New York City, where, after two years of study, I became an Ordained Interfaith Minister. Today, through my coaching practice, I work with clients on connecting with their inner magic and authentic self. We dig deep and together excavate and discard limiting paradigms that are keeping them from experiencing a rich and vibrant life. They learn to focus on the present and future—and let go of the past—with intent and desire. I help extraordinary individuals learn to dream big—bigger than they ever imagined and create the life of their dreams; one filled with creativity, joy, and well-being.

As I was preparing to graduate from seminary, I sold my house. I felt it was time to downsize and create a new garden. When I visited the last time, I felt strangely calm until I entered the garden. As soon as I walked through the back arbor, tears began forming. I said good-bye to the red velvet rose bush sprawling across the wall which I had bought decades earlier for only a few dollars. Every few steps I stopped, cradled some plants in my hands, and bid them adieu, telling them, like children, to take care of each other. Perhaps someone watching might think I'd gone crazy, but I knew otherwise. These beautiful living things were so deeply connected to me, and I to them, that parting was exquisitely painful.

The pain, though, proved to be a prelude to wonderful changes. I'm now gardening on an urban rooftop halfway across the world and am blessed with two separate areas where I can continue planting my perennials and vegetables. Gardening in a Mediterranean climate, in a much smaller space, offers its share of challenges. But it also comes with some wonderful benefits: I often have sunflowers blooming through December, and my first batch of mouthwatering, sweet tomatoes in the spring can ripen as early as May. I've also learned, once again, that if you build it, they will come. My garden is filled with bees, butterflies, and birds—evidence that by following the lead of nature and creating the right habitat, these lovely and much-needed creatures will be drawn to visit.

Thoughts for the Future

As I write this, I'm sitting in an apartment overlooking the magnificent and lush greenery of Rittenhouse Square in Philadelphia. I returned to Philly this past spring to celebrate my dad's 90th birthday and to help start a community garden in an economically challenged area in West Philadelphia. It's been both a beautiful and humbling experience.

My once-athletic father now holds my hand on our daily walks through the square because he's too frail to walk on his own. For the first time ever, we sit on a park bench and chat as we watch people sitting quietly or talking, enjoy dogs and children at play, and observe nature. Although my father doesn't comment on the beauty that surrounds him, I know he's taking it in. Because of this magnificent park, he and I are connecting in a way that we never have before. I've sat with him dozens of times this summer, glancing at him with tears in my eyes, thinking to myself, "These moments will become cherished memories."

Without my faith and profound connection to nature, I might find it painful to see my father's capabilities diminishing. But thanks to my years of being in tune with the rhythms of the earth, for me, there is a beauty and naturalness to how his last years are taking shape. After all, we, like the flowers in the garden, are destined to die and return to the earth. That knowledge infuses me with a feeling of peacefulness and a deep serenity.

We're presently living through tumultuous and unsettling times, and often we feel disconnected, lost, and scared. Clients frequently tell me they feel like they're running on a treadmill, going nowhere. Now more than ever, we need the tools of gardening and connecting with nature to ground us in a healthy reality—one where we feel alive, open, grateful, and with the ability to focus on the stuff that truly matters. It's through connecting with our most authentic self and nature that we develop the tools to create our own deeply meaningful reality.

I believe that gardeners, and others who are connected to nature, treat the land with kindness and love, and that directly translates into treating ourselves and each other with kindness and love. Although some might not admit it, we tend to be an optimistic tribe. Otherwise, why would we spend countless hours in the fall planting hundreds of bulbs which we have to wait until next spring to see bloom? Or what would possess us to buy a small tree that we know won't reach maturity for another twenty years? It's because we have faith in the future and want to play a small role in helping to create and maintain a healthy and beautiful planet for our children and future generations.

As in any art form or ritual, practice takes you to a deeper, richer, and more competent zone. So it is with gardening. I encourage you to make it a priority in your life and do as much of it as you can. If you only have fifteen minutes in the morning to do a bit of weeding before jumping into a hectic day, take your cup of coffee with you into the garden and go for it. Those fifteen minutes of connecting with your garden and getting your hands in the earth will do more for your soul than you can possibly imagine. It's an ideal time to practice mindfulness, clear out the clutter in your brain, and just be with nature.

For non-gardeners, even if you choose not to get your hands in the dirt right now, you can benefit from spending time outside surrounded by green. Whether you take a walk or sit in a park, be silent and be present. Observe and breathe in nature. Return to

Digging Deep as a guide to help you work on strengthening your creativity muscles. There's no rush in trying to make big changes. Bite-size changes actually build better habits. But be dogged in your approach. My advice is to address one or, at most, two, and you'll be surprised how quickly you'll gain traction and see positive changes in your daily life.

Our culture views gardening as a hobby. I urge you to give it the deference it deserves. Through gardening, we develop a spiritual relationship with nature. When we tend to a piece of land or to a plant, we're participating in the most magnificent dance of all. Although it may look as if we're the caretakers, like in any healthy, long-standing relationship, we receive as much, if not more, than we give.

Gardening is about creating community, abundance, beauty, and love. From working in the garden regularly, we learn to revere nature as our mentor, teacher, and guide. Simply put, nature is a life force, and gardening is a profound way to connect with it. It heals us, others, and the world, and is an essential tool for living an authentic, creative, and joyful life.

Introduction

What does it mean to be creative?

Does it mean to paint a gorgeous painting, to write a novel, compose a symphony, or design a skyscraper? To some degree, yes. Creativity is needed for all of these. Certainly these pursuits are artful and noble, but there is also a much wider meaning and purpose to creativity that touches the edges of every single one of our lives.

Creativity is very simply the energy of making something new where there was nothing before, and we have the potential to do this every day, in so many unmarked ways—from designing our schedules to fashioning our "look," from writing birthday cards to building a business from the ground up. Lawyers create arguments, lovers create romance, advertisers create pitches, decorators create ambiance, and parents create everything from learning games to a sense of wonder for their children. Every time we get dressed, make dinner, or wrap a gift, we can be creative. In almost everything we do in life, we have the possibility of conjuring up the spirit of inspiration, imagination, innovation, and resourcefulness.

There are many resources out there that can teach you how to do all these things and more, but what we're aiming to get at in this book is not simply being specifically creative in terms of a project, but also generally creative in terms of how we approach life. Creativity is not something we do; it is something we embody. I believe the ultimate goal is not to *be more creative*, but to learn how *to live creatively*.

Living creatively means approaching each moment as an opportunity to be spontaneous. It means opening to possibility, exploring, trusting your instincts, and owning and expressing your unique style. It means being true to your needs, experimenting, taking risks, staying flexible, and not always having to rush to conclusion. A person living creatively is always pushing towards new growth, as the psychologist Rollo May says, not *without* fear, but *in spite of it.*

This kind of creativity is accessed from within, and every single one of us has it. Perhaps you believe *I'm just not creative.* Oh, how many times I have heard that! But if you are like any of the countless people I have heard utter that familiar refrain, I promise you are mistaken. There's no such thing as a person born without creativity. Have you ever seen a child refuse to color with crayons, claiming they aren't creative? Of course not! Every single one of us has a creative spirit— it's just a question of whether we've had the opportunity or inkling to nurture it as the years have gone by.

Living creatively does more than just make things around us prettier or wittier. Our creative roots make up the very fiber of who we are as individuals, and by unearthing our creative nature, we at the same time unearth our authentic selves—not the persona we offer to the world, and not who we think we ought to be, but who we are in our deepest realms. As we create, we begin to reveal ourselves until one day we realize that who we really are and what we are doing are in perfect alignment. At the end of the day, the reason we create is not for the finished product, but to get to the best parts of ourselves.

Creativity and Gardening

I have a mission. My mission is not to have everyone create world-class gardens or to be the foremost expert on gardening. There are plenty of wonderful teachers out there who fulfill those needs. My mission is to show new and experienced gardeners alike how they can use their gardens—be they rolling, manicured lawns or tiny, blank plots of land—as tools for their creative awakening. I believe from the depths of my heart that gardening can be one of the most profound ways to unearth the creative spirit buried within every one of us. Once you unleash this creative energy, you'll be amazed at what happens in all areas of your life. You'll begin to see how living creatively opens up new vistas in your imagination and new windows of opportunity in your life.

I remember a client from years ago named Claire who lived in an older Victorian house and hired me to help her design the property around her home. Actually, she thought she hired me to design her garden for her, but she was in for a surprise. I told her we were going to create her dream garden together, at which she visibly balked.

"Oh, I can't do that!" Claire told me in no uncertain terms. "I have absolutely no idea what I would want in my garden! I figured you would just come and plant some things for me."

I assured Claire that together we would piece together what her dream garden might look like. She was skeptical, but agreed to spend the next week perusing through magazines and books to choose elements, colors, and styles that resonated for her. I gave her this exercise to help her expand her vision, train her eye to what she authentically liked and didn't like, and inspire herself (you'll be doing this yourself later on in Stage One).

When I returned a week later, Claire met me at the door with a huge smile on her face, practically hopping up and down with excitement. While going through several of the books I suggested on cottage gardens, a whole world of possibilities and feelings of *I want that!* exploded her inside. She remembered a long-lost love of hanging swings, like the one she had outside her childhood home. She had completely forgotten how much she adored passing lazy summer afternoons on that swing until a picture in a magazine beckoned to her.

When she showed me what she had done, and I told her we could incorporate many of the elements she liked into her garden—including a two-seater swing hanging from a large willow tree in the backyard—she got even more energized and happily immersed herself in envisioning her garden. It didn't take long for Claire and me to work through the specifics of what she wanted, and within a few weeks, the garden she saw in her mind's eye began to take shape in reality.

A few months later, Claire called me to say that the experience she had designing and planting her garden gave her a whole new outlook. She realized that if she could bring to fruition the garden vision of her dreams, perhaps she could create magic in other areas of her life, as well. She had never forgotten her long-ago dream of starting a catering business, and she was now in the process of planning her one-woman company as a result of experiencing firsthand the inspiring and fulfilling process of creating.

Every single one of us is unique, which is why I don't teach gardening-by-numbers. That's mimicking, the equivalent of folks tracing another artist's work and calling it their own. Why would you want to garden like me, when you can garden like *you*? The goal is to get to the roots of what is original within your heart and soul, and to find your original style, the style that shines directly from who you authentically are. The key to living a meaningful life is to set out on the path to discovering all that is under your surface, and gardening is a wonderful forum in which to do this. It's a very wise and forgiving medium, this earth of ours.

It doesn't matter whether you have a twenty-acre plot of land or a fire escape in the back of a city apartment; *gardening with intent* is not about how much space you have. It's about being mindful, staying in the present moment, and being attentive to what you're doing. In its simplest form, gardening is simply the process of actively relating with some sort of plant life. I have a few elderly ladies come to my workshops who have only African violets on their coffee tables, but they are emotionally invested in caring for these little plants. By all means, these ladies are gardening!

No matter who you are, how creative you hold yourself to be, or how big or small your garden, gardening can be a profound method of discovering and reconnecting to your authentic roots and ultimately growing into the self-actualized person you're destined to be. I believe this so strongly because I've not only seen it happen to hundreds of my clients, like Claire, but also felt and seen these changes occur within myself.

My Story

I wasn't born an expert gardener, and, like so many people I know, I spent many years afraid of my own creativity—my own aliveness. I hid from so much of what was vital and unique about me in order to fit in and succeed in a world that puts a premium on conformity and external success. Until one day, upon gazing out at the completely blank yard of what was then my brand-new home, I realized I was too terrified to even begin to imagine what to do with it. The idea of having to "create"—to make something where there was nothing before—seemed completely overwhelming and impossible.

When I was in my late twenties, I moved with my husband and two small children into a newly constructed home surrounded only by dirt. Ours was the first home to be built in this new neighborhood, and I thought the piece of property we'd chosen at the far end of a cul-de-sac would be the perfect place to raise our kids. The builders let us know that the backyard would be gently sloping, which honestly meant basically nothing to me at the time. I figured I would do what I had always done when it came to landscaping—either add a few things to what was already there or hire a professional to do it for me. I'd had some gardening experience at that point (childhood gardening chores, dozens of houseplants around my dorm room in college, and maintaining the garden at our first home), so it wasn't a big deal to me. I'd grown up with a mom who was always fiddling around outside, transplanting things and cutting flowers to bring in from the garden, but I certainly never thought gardening would be the path that would ultimately change my life.

When the last bulldozer pulled away and the final touches were completed on our home, I gazed at the property in dismay. Never did I envision that the ground would be completely bare—with nary a flower or tree in sight! It was barren and ugly, not to mention dangerous. The "gentle slope" we had been told about turned out to be a steep incline up the backyard; one good rainstorm and we would have a mudslide right through our kitchen. What was supposed to be the home of my dreams turned out to be the property of my nightmares.

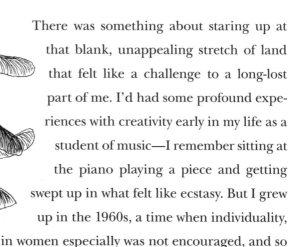

There was something about staring up at that blank, unappealing stretch of land that felt like a challenge to a long-lost part of me. I'd had some profound experiences with creativity early in my life as a student of music—I remember sitting at the piano playing a piece and getting swept up in what felt like ecstasy. But I grew up in the 1960s, a time when individuality, in women especially was not encouraged, and so I put my energies where I would get rewarded: being popular and social and getting good grades. In college, I studied psychology and creativity (they say we are always pulled towards what we most need to learn!) under such renowned researchers and teachers as Erika Fromm. Though I was fluent in the theories about creativity, I was pretty clueless when it came to personal application.

At some point along the way, I made the decision that the path to my personal freedom was to be financially solvent, and made an unconscious decision to follow the male model of power. I got into broadcast media and eventually became a media trainer, which was very lucrative but not really all that personally satisfying. I knew something was missing; I just didn't know quite what it was. I felt bound and constricted inside, completely confused about what the yearning inside me was for.

So, here I was in a new home, in a new neighborhood, with two young children, feeling frustrated, unhappy, and uncreative. I knew I needed to make this place my own, so I started with something familiar. Convinced I had no taste, I hired a decorator to furnish our home. This decorator was a lovely man who also happened to be a passionate gardener. He would bring me armloads of daylilies to plant in my yard or an old book on gardening and would urge me to plant a few things here and there, which I did, without any real sense of what I was doing. But he continued to cajole me, and slowly, little by little, I got out there and planted a few rose bushes, then some evergreens, petunias, and so on.

When I look at how I planted things back then, I'm amazed that anything survived, but the point was that I was getting my hands in the dirt. In hindsight, I now understand why I kept on gardening, even though I didn't know what I was doing. The feeling of my hands in the dirt offered me such a deep, primordial connection with the earth. When I was working the earth, I was at peace. It felt so right and so good. I know that sounds trite, but it's the truth. The biblical phrase "from the earth we come and to the earth we go" started to have a whole new relevance for me.

There was also something profound about tending these precious plants and seeing them grow. I remember planting petunias on a terraced area in the backyard, loving the feeling of digging that hole of freshly prepared, crumbly soil, of placing the plant in the hole and tamping the soil around it to make sure that it was secure and snug in its new home. I loved watering these new flowers with my watering can, and I remember each day coming outside to check on them with anticipation. With their growth, something within me started to come alive. I started to feel the familiar stirrings—the sparks inside that playing the piano had awakened so many years before.

One day I passed what I thought was a private home in an estate area near me. It had magnificent pink antique roses climbing a wrought-iron fence out front, and beyond was a vivid and sprawling wildflower meadow. Of course, I stopped the car and pulled over—this was breathtaking! When I got home, I called my gardening pal in the neighborhood (who was much more advanced than I and had turned me onto several great gardening catalogs) and asked her about this home. She told me it was a private estate run by an English gardener by the name of Christopher Woods. Well, when I want something, I go after it, so I tracked down Chris, who ultimately became my teacher and the person who inspired me to go to England and study garden making in earnest.

Under his tutelage, I learned the necessary basics, and step-by-step my garden started to take shape. I planted flowers and trees, laid beds only to rip them back up again and try something else. I had literally tons of dirt carted away to even out the steep slope in the back of the house, completely redoing the entire structure of the property. I will never forget what one of my dearest friends said to me when she came by and saw what I was doing: "Frannie, how can you do this? You are literally unearthing the foundation on which you live!"

She was right. I was unearthing everything—including the fear and trepidation that had bound me for so many years. I started to trust my instincts, to pay attention to what I knew would work for me, and to take some real risks and be willing to make mistakes. Though of course the story is much more complex than can be summed up in a few paragraphs, I started to notice changes going on within me right along with my evolving garden.

I learned to live with ambiguity and to not always rush to conclusion. In the garden, sometimes you just have to wait and see what develops—something I was never all that good at in my personal life. I liked to know what was going to happen at all times. But I started to trust the process of life more, both in my plants and in myself. For instance, my daughter lives in Israel, which is not always the safest place to be in these troubled times, and whenever I hear of something else happening over there, my instinct is to call and say, "Come home, now!" But I have to remember that living there is what brings her joy, and that we simply don't know what will occur from one day to the next. I trust my daughter and know she takes every precaution; beyond that, I remind myself to be okay with not knowing what the future holds.

I saw myself become more fluid in the relationships that were close to me. With both my children and my spouse, I became more patient. By nature, I'm intense, but over time it became obvious to everyone around me that I was becoming calmer, less prone to emotional outbursts. I learned so much from my experience in my garden; not to etch in stone preconceived notions of what things will end up looking or feeling like (none of my gardens has *ever* ended up being anything like I thought it was going to be when I planned it), and that making mistakes is one of the greatest gifts available to us. I came to understand—and I mean *really* understand—that if I'm not making mistakes, then I'm not taking risks in the garden... and in life.

Perhaps the biggest lesson that gardening taught me was that I, Fran Sorin, or we, human beings, are not in charge. Much as we like to think we control everything, we don't. There's a force much greater than us. Nature, God, call it what you will, but it's there. I learned this because I saw repeatedly that I could do everything right—plant a healthy plant in good soil, water it, fertilize it, tend it—and it still might not survive. Talk about learning acceptance!

Over a period of ten years, I evolved from a scared beginner to a person confident and at home in my garden. Someone got wind of my garden and recommended that it be included on a Philadelphia horticulture tour. One thing led to another and I began doing gardening features on the local Fox TV station and hands-on workshops for the Pennsylvania Horticultural Society. Then came more features on Lifetime and The Discovery Channel, and eventually I became NBC's *Weekend Today Show* regular gardening expert. Meanwhile, I helped to develop the Gardening Channel on iVillage.com and began to write articles for a variety of national publications. Finally, I was asked to host my own weekly gardening talk radio show for Infinity Broadcasting. My garden design business was just a natural evolution as people started to come to me for advice, and here I am.

When clients come to me to help them create their gardens, I let them know up front that it's not something that I'm going to do *for* them, just like I told Claire all those years ago. It's something we do together. I can't get inside the heart and mind of my clients; it's up to them to dig deep and learn to hone their powers of envisioning, dreaming, experimenting, problem solving, and taking risks. What I can do is teach them the essential gardening basics (without which all experimenting is just arbitrary), then work with them as we go through my seven-stage process of awakening their creative spirits in the garden. It doesn't take long for the clients' dream gardens to emerge as they begin to break free of their fears and constraints and begin to let go and create. One of the greatest privileges of my life is to witness these gardeners bloom right along with their garden.

How to Use *Digging Deep*

What I hope to do in this book is take you through my Seven Stages of Creative Awakening within the context of your garden: Imagining, Envisioning, Planning, Planting, Tending, Enjoying, and Completing. You'll learn all you need to know to design the garden of your dreams—even if you have no idea what that garden is right now—but that's just the tip of the iceberg. A magnificent, thriving garden is the by-product of a magnificent, thriving gardener, and really, this is all about *you*. The tulips and roses will be beautiful, but they'll pale in comparison to the inner glow you radiate once your creative fires have been lit.

You can either read this book the entire way through and follow the stages in order, or you can dip in as you choose and go right to the stage that best applies to where you are at this particular time. You'll notice that many of the themes loop in and throughout the different stages, and this is because creating is not a linear process. Like a Chinese jump rope, we weave in, out, and through the various pathways, and every single time the configuration is different.

In each section, there are experiments for you to try. If you're a beginner, these exercises will help build your confidence and allow you to start accessing and expressing what's in your imagination. If you're already an experienced gardener, pick and choose from the sections that most call to you, to bring a new, awakened perspective to your gardening. Throughout, I'll give advice and tips about the "how-tos," which are the foundations of any healthy and sound garden.

Together, we'll design and plant your garden and wake up your creative nature. Before long, I am certain you'll find that you begin to flourish. Perhaps you'll be like Peter, a computer salesperson who came to me (or so he thought!) to learn how to care for his lawn, but ended up discovering a passion for designing and building rock gardens. Within three months of designing and building a beautiful rock garden of his own, he noticed that he was thinking more innovatively at work, thus opening the door to more sales opportunities.

Maybe you will have something in common with Maria, a diminutive, conservative woman to whom I recommended my *Playing with Flowers* exercise in which you go to the store and buy as many fresh-cut flowers as you can, come home, pull out all the vases and containers in your home, put on music you love, and just *play* (you'll do this exercise in Stage One). Experimenting with color so inspired her that she actually gave away a good portion of her boring, drab clothes and, trusting her newfound eye and instinct for color, put together a whole new, vibrant wardrobe for herself.

Or maybe you'll relate to the experience of Leslie, who brought me in to consult on planting rosebushes and soon found herself using the petals of her deliciously fragrant roses to blend her own line of scented bath oils. Who knows what you'll discover within yourself once you unearth your creative roots?

One thing is for certain, however: You will never again question whether you are creative. You will know beyond a shadow of a doubt that once you discover your authentic, creative nature, you can create absolutely anything you dare to in and of your life.

Imagining

The Sparks of Creativity

To imagine is to see possibilities, to envision realities that don't yet exist, and map out secret paths not yet charted. Our imaginations are our own personal mental playgrounds, where we release our dreams to romp without risk or fear. It is here, in the inner regions of our psyches, that we are free to explore who we truly are and let our thoughts and wishes run wild. It's here that we cook up all our fantasies, our deepest desires, and, very often, all the hopes and longings that we never share with another living soul. It's from this wellspring that we draw the inspiration that serves as the spark for our creative fires.

When I was a little girl, I had a wild imagination. I spun all sorts of ideas and fantasies around in my head that would brim over into impromptu theatrical performances. I exclaimed! I bemoaned! I exalted! I felt so much and expressed it all. My mother nicknamed me Talullah, after the legendary actress and diva Tallullah Bankhead, if that gives you any idea of what I was like. But somehow I got the message as a child that it wasn't good to be that way: that I shouldn't let out all my emotions and imaginings for all the world to see. My teachers would often sigh with exasperation and say, "Oh, Frannie, what are we going to do with you?"

I had no one with whom I could share my excitement over very important matters like finding a fuzzy caterpillar clinging to the windowsill outside my bedroom, or how much fun it was to try on my mother's high heels and parade down the makeshift catwalk I constructed in our suburban living room, so out of the overspill of imagination, I created an equally ecstatic imaginary friend named Locky Lee Boom Boom. Locky Lee and I would have fabulous tea parties and make endless lists of boys we liked, exotic places we planned to visit one day, and whom we would thank when we won our first Academy Award. Locky Lee was always right there, ready to play in whatever scenario I could dream up.

Somehow, life gives us the message loud and clear that imagination is a Sunday-afternoon luxury that we should put away as we mature. As many of us grow up and add on degrees and jobs and all the other stuff that is part of life, we bid farewell to our Locky Lee Boom Booms and dreams of distant memory and do what the world signals as necessary: look ahead, set goals, stick to the game plan. It's the rare few who are able—or who dare—to retain that childlike sense of wonder and become what we eventually call artistic, creative, gifted. Sometimes we even call them weird. But secretly, we sense they are somehow better off than we—perhaps happier, more blessed. They aren't any different than us, really, except in one fundamental way: Their imaginations refused to be pushed underground. They live of and through their dreams, not through effort, but by nature.

The most miraculous thing about imagination is that it never dies, no matter how many layers of life and work we pile on top of it. The opportunity to revisit and rekindle our dreams and imaginative powers is always there. Imagination isn't something we have to cultivate; it is who we are in our most private realms, and all we need to do to access it is open the internal windows and set it free. It's there in every single one of us. I promise! I have seen even the most buttoned-down, serious types come alive like a little kid in their gardens once they let themselves go and start to play.

Martin, for instance, was one of my first clients. He brought me in to design the landscaping of his new home, which was purchased for him by his employer when they moved him and his family from Chicago. Martin was all business: We met at 8:30 A.M. sharp, and he let me know right away what the budget was and how soon he expected the work to be completed. I can still remember the look on his face when I said, "OK, then, why don't we start by talking a little bit about what you imagine for this space?"

I could tell this wasn't on Martin's agenda, but I had been referred to him by his new boss, so I think he felt he had to go along with the program. He took off his jacket, sat down at the kitchen table with me, and we started to talk about different ideas. At first Martin was reluctant to say much, but I sensed there was something under there, so I pressed. And guess what? Within forty-five minutes, Martin had pulled out a box of his son's colored pencils and was excitedly sketching out "just a few thoughts" he had. It was amazing to watch the transformation: The hard lines of his face softened, and his whole body seemed looser and more relaxed as he drew. Two hours later, when he walked me to the door, I would swear I was shaking the hand of a whole other person than I met on the way in.

A garden can be a wonderful place to reopen the window to your imagination, especially when it isn't yet a garden at all, but rather a blank space that you hope to transform into a garden. An untouched piece of land is such pure opportunity, just like a clean canvas or a fresh piece of white paper. In its nakedness, it's raw possibility. Onto it, you can project any vision or wish you like, continually erasing and trying new mental pictures, again and again.

This initial stage is about sparking our creative memories, opening ourselves up to a sense of freedom and possibility, awakening the stirrings of play and spontaneity. The only thing you need to do from the outset is to commit to not having any agenda and not worrying about what will work and what won't work. There's nothing to figure out here—nothing you need to accomplish, no puzzle you need to solve. You can't claim your imaginative powers through force. A sense of wonder is not something to achieve, but rather something to awaken, moment by precious moment.

Even Albert Einstein, whose very name has become synonymous with brilliance and intelligence, once remarked, "Imagination is more important than knowledge."

Observing

"If you truly love nature,
you will find beauty everywhere."

—Vincent Van Gogh

Observing is simply the act of consciously attending to or making note of something. In the fast-paced world we inhabit in the twenty-first century, so many of us move through our days as if blindfolded. We race from one item on our to-do list to the next, hurriedly trying to get it all done better and quicker, barely taking notice of that which is around us. It is not our fault, really—it's just the way our world works. But this hectic pace comes at a price. We may be able to do everything, but how much space does that leave to truly and deeply *experience* anything? Though we may not know it, we are slowly becoming alienated from a primary source of our creativity: our senses.

Observing is the polar opposite of that. It means tapping all our senses to really see, feel, taste, smell, and touch the world around us in such a way that we reconnect with our sensuality. We awaken our aesthetic intelligence, our appreciation for beauty, harmony, melody, aroma, and sensation—all of which illuminate our imaginative energies and serve as the palette from which we can draw. Observing the natural world around us is one of the simplest ways to begin to awaken our senses and stimulate our creative fires.

When we forget to stay alert, we start to take nature for granted, slowly disassociating from it and, ultimately, from ourselves. But when we look around us with keen, clear eyes and wide-open ears, we start noticing people, places, and things in whole new ways. Really, if you think about it, all great poetry is created out of a heightened sense of awareness. Here is how it happens: The poet comes into contact with a source of inspiration, be it a pinecone or the graceful curve of his lover's bare shoulder. He has what psychologist Rollo May calls an "encounter," which is a moment of becoming profoundly inspired and completely absorbed in something. Out of this encounter, he is moved to articulate the very essence of his experience, which comes forth in the form of mellifluous poetry. Yet none of this would have been more than a fleeting moment of lost opportunity had the poet not been so receptive to his senses in the first place.

You may have passed by the same patch of wildflowers day after day on your way to work, but if you consciously pause to take it in, you bring it into sharper focus and may experience it differently. Maybe this time you'll feel the silky petals, soft as cashmere; or see the reds, fiery and vibrant as a late-summer sunset, or the brilliant yellows that remind you of the joyful freedom of picking buttercups as a child. Anything can happen when you wake up your senses. It doesn't have to be poetry that you're seeking to create. My friend Susan is a litigator and is one of the most creative people I know, though she's never written a single sonnet, played a note, or lifted a paintbrush. Susan creates in the courtroom, crafting brilliant positions and solid arguments where before there was only speculation and uncertainty.

I can be just as guilty as the next person of forgetting to stay present and slipping into that semislumber. Like most people, I have a very busy life. There's my garden to tend, clients to consult with, articles to write, deadlines to meet, workshops to organize—and that's just the work part of my life. I love my friends dearly and try to make time to be with them to share a cup of tea and our thoughts, not to mention my two grown children. All this can add up to the proverbial "no time to smell the roses." Whenever I start to feel overwhelmed and exhausted, I know I've lost touch with my senses and with myself. It means nothing if my gardens win all the awards in the world if I'm not present to the brilliant purple of the clematis, or the wisteria's heavenly scent, or the sweet tinkling of the wind chime in the chilly December wind. At the end of the day, that reminder to stay ever present to nature is the reason I garden.

There is something so very deep—so very primal—about humankind's connection to nature. It is here, in our honest engagement with the natural world, that we connect to our most essential humanness. Nature isn't a hobby. It's part of us and we're part of it. We're an extension of the ecosystem, which is why I find it so interesting when I hear people say they aren't "into nature." We can be no more "into nature" than we can be "into breathing." We exist in tandem with the natural world. Everything we eat originates in nature: vegetables, fruits, plants, animals, herbs. Many of our references—even those we may never even think about—come from nature. For instance, names like Lily, Iris, Rose, Holly, Heather, or familiar aphorisms, such as "the apple doesn't fall far from the tree," "forget me not," and "shrinking violet." Yet so many of us close ourselves off from nature, not unlike the way we close ourselves off from our authentic roots.

The process of unearthing who and what we are begins by embracing our part in the greater force at work all around us.

When you see your favorite frog back in the pond after a long winter, it's a reunion of sorts. One of my workshop students told of a beautiful dogwood tree outside the window of her childhood bedroom. For so many years, she observed that tree through every season, noticing how it shed its leaves every winter only to burst into bloom with creamy pink and white flowers when spring arrived. No matter what was going on in her life, or what growing pains she might be going through, that tree always came to life every April to remind her of new beginnings. She saw how nature is the most consistently reliable companion each of us maintains throughout our lives. Come what may, the seasons will change, the birds will migrate, snowflakes will fall, bulbs will bloom from the soil, the sun will rise and set. We can count on all of this, even when everything else around us seems so uncertain.

Being in nature—really being there, not just passing through—can provide us with a profound sense of peace and belonging. Our problems may suddenly seem small and insignificant as we recognize the bigger picture in play all around us. An inflated sense of self-importance starts to seem ridiculous when we realize our community is not just limited to our family, friends, colleagues... it is a community of all living things.

I always say that nature is the great equalizer. No part of our ecosystem is ultimately more important or more valuable than another, including us. You may struggle with being the master or mistress of your domain, but when you're in the garden, you're no more esteemed than the ladybug! There is an interconnectedness all around us that, if we are willing to tune in to it, can continually remind us to keep things in perspective.

You don't need to travel to the Grand Canyon or to the jungles of Central America to observe astonishing displays of nature. They are accessible to every single one of us, right in our own yard or on our street. It doesn't matter whether you live on twenty acres or in a city apartment; nature is all around you, available for you to take in at any time.

The whole process of creativity is about coming alive and interacting in an inspired way with the world around you, and observation is where it all starts. The very acts of consciously touching, listening, smelling, and sensing open the doors to heightened awareness, out of which you can begin to deeply till the fertile soil of your creative spirit.

 To try

To begin with, get a blank journal, which will serve throughout this process as your Nature Journal. Take your time in making your choice. You want to buy a journal that speaks to you and that you find aesthetically pleasing (and, of course, that's easy to write in).

Once you have your journal, I strongly encourage you to begin taking what I call "nature walks." They're a designated twenty to thirty minutes each day in which you walk outdoors, slow down, take some deep breaths, become mindful of the beauty surrounding you, and notice in detail at least one aspect of nature. It might be a solitary autumn leaf on the ground, aflame with red and gold, or the weeds struggling to grow through a crack in the sidewalk, or even the scent of wood smoke from a nearby fire. Stop and look at one single flower up close. There's a whole universe in the plush center of a sunflower! Run your hands over the bark of a tree. Take off your shoes and walk across your front lawn, even if—especially if—people tend not to do such things in your neighborhood. Pay attention to the sights, sounds, and scents that you encounter, and the feelings these sensations evoke in you. When you come in from your nature walk, take a few minutes to record in your journal what you've observed, being as detailed as possible.

Sometimes on my nature walks, I like to choose one particular thing, like a specific tree or a certain flower, to check in with every day. This way, I can witness all its tiny changes each day, up close, just as I did with my children as they grew day by day. Try this to see how it feels to foster a sense of intimacy and familiarity with one small piece of nature. It's also a wonderful way to practice mindfulness, of being attentive to what you're experiencing.

I encourage you to continue your nature walks throughout this entire process. Though it may seem like a small action, you're actually taking great strides in awakening your senses each time you do it. Further, by observing the myriad options and changes in nature around you, you'll probably start to identify elements that you'll want to incorporate into your garden—your own personal wonder of nature.

GREAT MINDS THINK ALIKE...

- ✧ Beethoven composed much of his work while strolling about in nature.

- ✧ Darwin's theory of evolution was greatly influenced by the many hours he spent observing the flora and fauna in his garden.

- ✧ Leonardo da Vinci never had any formal schooling or training—he claimed he learned everything he knew about life, design, structure, and art simply by observing nature.

- ✧ Winston Churchill often sat for hours observing his beloved garden, searching for inspiration and solace during some of his most challenging times in office.

Discovering

"To perceive freshly, with fresh senses,
is to be inspired."

—Henry David Thoreau

Often the scariest question to answer can be, *What do I want?* The sheer open-ended boundlessness can be overwhelming. The choices seem so vast that it feels practically impossible to land on anything at all. That's why restaurants have menus. Can you imagine walking into a restaurant, sitting down, and having the waiter ask you out of the blue, "So, what would you like?" Without an array of specific options to whet your appetite and spark a sense of desire, you might very likely have no clue what you want to eat.

When I first started my garden design business, I would meet with new clients and begin by asking them what kinds of gardens and plant life they liked. A rookie mistake, for sure, because more often than not my question was met with one of two responses: a blank stare, or a look of mild panic. Here these lovely people were hiring me to help them design their gardens, and I was asking them right off the bat to articulate everything they wanted and didn't want. It didn't take too long for me to figure out that the process began not with a direct and decisive game plan, but rather with the very tender and precious process of learning what they authentically felt drawn towards.

So many of us really have no idea what it is that we deeply and personally want. I used to work with a woman named Donna who separated from her husband when she was thirty-eight. When Donna moved into her new apartment on her own, she looked around at the empty space with dread. All her life, she had lived in homes that had basically been decorated for her: first by her mother when she was growing up, and later, when she was married, by a professional interior decorator. Now, for the first time in her life, she had the opportunity to create a space just for herself, and she had no idea where to begin. Though she was a very outwardly successful media personality by this time, she was a bit lost when it came to finding her way around her interior terrain.

"It was crazy," Donna later told me, recalling that time. "I was thirty-eight years old and had absolutely no clue what I liked—what style was really *me*. I knew what was considered 'tasteful,' but I could barely begin to fathom what appealed to me and what didn't."

But Donna is the intrepid sort, so it didn't take long for the dread to turn into determination. She figured if she had the courage to leave a marriage that wasn't working for her and start fresh, she could for sure do a little more internal digging and discover her aesthetic desires. She started slowly, flipping through catalogs and magazines, visiting showrooms and furniture stores, flea markets and auctions, to see what sparked her interest and what turned her off. Slowly, she began making choices and filling in her apartment, one small step at a time.

"What was so amazing," she remembered, "was that I really didn't know what was going to come out of me. I just started and figured I'd see what happened. I didn't know what I was going to end up with—it could have very easily become a hodgepodge of a mess!"

It was far from a mess. I remember the first time I visited her apartment, about six months after she moved in. I could hardly believe it: Here was Donna, my tough-as-nails friend who took no bull from anyone, living in an apartment adorned with lovely Queen Anne-style furniture, vintage lace curtains, and an exquisite antique writing table. I'll never forget what she said to me when I stood there looking around in wonder:

"Yep... love that frilly girly stuff. Who knew?"

As a result of her happy fascination with antiques and all things pretty, Donna is quite content spending her weekends scouting out flea markets and shops that sell hand-embroidered linens, china, and the like. She eventually pitched a pilot to her producer about the often hilarious world of collecting, of which she will be the host. Through her desires, she has fashioned a truly authentic life that feeds her, heart and soul.

Discovering your wishes is one of the most basic ways to begin unearthing your authentic roots. In order to create anything that has true resonance for you, you must first know what really calls to you. Otherwise, you're just casting about, dabbling with this or that—a process from which you may or may not create a solution. Certainly whatever end you come to might work just fine, but what was truly gained in the process? Did you learn anything about yourself? Have you grown as a result?

In the garden, there are literally thousands of options that you can incorporate. It can be quite overwhelming. So these days, instead of asking my clients point-blank what they want, I guide them through the following activity. Try it...you may be surprised at what calls to you.

 *To try*

Get your hands on any gardening or home magazines that you can. Some of my favorite publications include *Gardens Illustrated*, *Architectural Digest*, *Domino*, *Country Living*, *Fine Gardening*, *Garden Design*, *Horticulture*, *Real Simple*, *House Beautiful*, and *Martha Stewart Living*.

Set aside a designated amount of time and begin to browse through and earmark anything that grabs your fancy that relates to the garden. It can be flowers, an actual garden bed, a type of tree, a structure such as a fountain or pergola, or just the overall look and feel of a garden. Tear out anything at all that calls to you. Don't censor yourself here—there are no rules. Just have fun. Pick and choose and rip out as you feel inclined. Take breaks if you need to. You don't need to cram a whole garden's worth of inspirations into one afternoon.

Pinterest.com is a fantastic resource for discovering what elements of a garden light you up. Using Pinterest's search function, you have thousands of photographs at your fingertips. Just type in what you'd like to explore, whether a general topic such as perennials or vegetable gardening, or something specific such as garden furniture or stone garden pathways. When you find things you like, simply click on the "Pin it" button to place the images into categories you've set up for easy access later on. It's an easy, playful, and plentiful way of accessing and organizing information.

If you can, I also encourage you to pick up a few gardening books that appeal to you. Go through the pages and put Post-its on the ones that you find particularly appealing, even if you don't know exactly why.

As you peruse and dream, try not to let the "how to" element sneak in. That's the censor of your mind trying to impose limits. People censor themselves so much, but this exercise is like brainstorming. Don't worry about what to do with the material or how you'll translate it into your own garden; just like what you like. We'll deal with pulling it all together later. For now, simply take pleasure in finding things that speak to you without having to give it structure or meaning, like the beginning of love.

We go into fear so quickly when we do exercises like this, because we immediately assume we have to have an agenda— a reason or a theme behind our likes or dislikes. We become frustrated... *I can't do this...this is impossible!* The key to unlocking this barrier is to recognize the frustration as simply *fear.* There's nothing you need to do about it, nothing you need to figure out, no problems to solve right now. Now is truly the fun part—just let go and dream!

This exercise will help you begin to see your likes and dislikes, thus allowing you to become more intimate with the longings within you. Being honest about your likes and dislikes frees you from the tyranny of *other people's opinions,* which can often cloud your authentic desires. Plus, reading through gardening magazines and books is a great way to learn the names and varieties of flowers you like, so that when the time comes to make those choices, you'll have a better sense of what's out there.

Keep the pictures that you find safely tucked away somewhere, because we'll be using them again later on in another exercise.

Remembering

*"God gave us memories that
we might have roses in December."*
—J.M. BARRIE

Our memories are rich sources of inspiration. In fact, memory is the treasure trove of material for most writers, for it is there that they store every sight, every sound, every feeling to later be used for a character or to draw a verbal picture.

Think—right now—of any positive aesthetic experience that has stuck with you. It can be a place, a view, the mood of a painting, the scent of your mother's homemade apple pie wafting from the kitchen on a crisp autumn afternoon. How does that memory make you feel? What does it evoke in you?

We all hold fond memories in our subconscious that shape who and what we come to love, and I find this to be especially true when it comes to gardens and nature. Gardens evoke a very strong response. It's primal, like the response to art or children. It's amazing how powerful our memories of nature can be, and pulling these memories to the surface gives us ownership of our sensibilities and what I call our "gardening consciousness." Our memories are integral to who we are, and the very act of bringing those remembered gardens to the surface gives us one more connection to the authentic roots within.

I have so many personal memories of gardens that have influenced what I love today. I remember clearly the experience of sitting in the back seat of my parents' Chevrolet as my father pulled up to our new home in Rochester, New York. I was eight years old at the time. The house was an older white clapboard situated on a deep lot with an ancient willow tree monopolizing the front yard. When I got out of the car, my leg grazed a flower that was planted in the island separating our property from the neighbors'. When I looked down to see what the feathery texture was brushing against my leg, I was overtaken by a beauty that I had never before experienced. It was a gorgeous magenta peony (though I didn't know the name of it at the time). I bent over to breathe in its luxurious scent, rapt with awe at the effect this flower had on me. I remember this moment as if it were yesterday. And when I first began to get into gardening in a keen way, what do you think I purchased with great abandon? Peonies, of course.

Over the years, I have encouraged clients to explore their own memory banks for similar memories. I have been privy to their stories about swinging on vines over backyard streams, watering potted geraniums on tiny urban fire escapes, woods where they made forts, and wide-open lawns on which they played Running Bases. One person recalled the scene in *The Wizard of Oz* when Dorothy and the Scarecrow wake up in a field of brilliant poppies (which just so happens to be one of my favorites, as well); another remembered collecting acorns with her early-childhood friends, pretending they were Laura Ingalls Wilder and needed to store up food for the winter. It's amazing what people remember.

Often people will say they can't remember anything at all at first, but eventually, incredibly clear memories will start to shine through. Vera, a workshop participant in her fifties, looked at me warily when I suggested this exercise. There was nothing in there to remember, she said. I told her that was fine; maybe she should just take a few days and see what surfaced. Sure enough, a few days later, Vera called and told me all about how she remembered picking raspberries out in a field behind her grandparents' farm in Connecticut. She recalled the delight of finding the fat, ripe berries that were ready for picking and how sweet the sticky juice tasted as she licked it off her fingers. She sounded so excited that I had to ask if she perhaps wanted to plant a few fruits and vegetables in her garden. The response? Yes!

To try ❀

Sit with your eyes closed and take three deep breaths. Think about some instances from your childhood when you connected with any element of nature. It could be a beautiful sight that took your breath away, being happily drenched in a sudden rainstorm, or the remembrance of the intoxicating aroma of a flower walking through a park on a summer evening.

Write down what you remember and how it made you feel. Try to connect with all of your senses when describing this moment: how it looked, felt, smelled, and what you might have heard. How does it make you feel today when you think about it?

If nothing comes to you at first, don't worry. Just sit with the questions for a little while, and I'm quite certain images will start to surface. Some may be quick snapshots, others full-blown images or scenes. Write your responses in as much detail as you can remember.

*What was the most memorable garden you
have ever come across? Think back, even if it was
in a movie, or a postcard, or a book...*

All this belongs to you—it is your reservoir of sensual experiences. The more you connect with what's in there, the more you'll be able to translate these preferences from the past into tangible realities in the present.

This exercise has tremendous value: Our childhood senses are our most primal, and by becoming reacquainted with these memories, we can dig a little deeper into what aspects of nature hold sincere meaning for us. We all have memories of beauty that transformed us, and by tapping into them, we can then find ways to surround ourselves with these sensations and emotions in our gardens today. Every time you enter your garden, it will be like visiting an old friend—a favorite and worn blanket, a dog-eared copy of your favorite book, the scent of your mother's floral perfume from years ago. These are the experiences that make our gardens so much more than pretty places; they transform them into living, breathing expressions of the memories woven into the fiber of who we are. ✿

Exploring

*"He leaped the fence, and saw that
all nature was a garden."*

—Horace Walpole

When was the last time you went exploring? Not hunting for something as we do when we go to a furniture store or a flea market searching for that one item we need, but exploring just for the sake of checking something out just to see what is there?

As you are beginning the process of teasing open your imagination, exploring can be a wonderful way to see possibilities that are out there that you might never have known about. For instance, Roger and Emily were newlyweds who bought a home in a lovely town in a suburb of Philadelphia. When I first met them, they said they wanted basically the same kind of front yard that the other houses in their neighborhood had: a brick walkway to the front door, some evergreen shrubs, some impatiens, and some mulch or gravel. When I asked them what it was about it that appealed to them, they looked at each other, then looked back at me and confessed that they really didn't know. Roger said he thought it looked nice, and Emily added that she had never really given any thought to landscaping—she just assumed they would do something harmonious with the other houses around them and leave it at that. She said she really would have no idea what any other options would look like.

I suggested that the two of them spend the following weekend exploring. They didn't need to travel far from home. I suggested they visit the Scott Arboretum and the Du Ponts' famous Longwood Gardens. The following Monday, Emily called and told me they had had a wonderful time wandering around and taking in the different gardens, and that they both fell madly in love with the rose garden at the Scott Arboretum. Together the three of us planned out a romantic and sumptuous rose garden for them in the front yard. Wouldn't you know that within a year, two of their neighbors called me to ask if I could come help them redo their front yards?

 *To try*

Go exploring. See what you like and what speaks to you. Wherever you live, I'm sure there are botanical gardens or public parks with gardens. Walk through and observe: What style gardens grab your attention? Which flowers take your breath away? Are there elements you see that you like, such as a small pond, brick walkways, or twig pergolas? Are you drawn to romantic and velvety leaves or to large bold, multi-colored ones? Another wonderful way to explore is to just get into your car and go for a drive. Look closely at the choices other people have made and ask yourself what you like and don't like about the results. Remember to record all of this in your Nature Journal; you'll want to refer to this information later in the process.

I think you'll find that once you start training your eyes in this way, every time you venture outside will be a new adventure. You'll start to look around in more observant and thoughtful ways, and may even get inspired to travel a bit outside your immediate realm and check out some gardens or nature preserves a bit further from home. There's a wide world out there of beautiful gardens to behold! 🌸

KEEP YOUR EYES OUT FOR GARDEN STRUCTURES THAT YOU LIKE...

❖ Pergolas ❖ Statues ❖ Gazebos

❖ Benches ❖ Arbors ❖ Fountains ❖ Stepping stones

❖ Windchimes ❖ Interesting antique pieces

SOME WONDERFUL GARDENS
TO EXPLORE

❖ *Chanticleer Gardens*, Wayne, Pennsylvania

❖ *New York Botanical Garden*, Bronx Park, New York

❖ *The High Line*, New York, New York

❖ *Fairchild Tropical Gardens*, Miami, Florida

❖ *Chicago Botanic Garden*, Glencoe, Illinois

❖ *Longwood Gardens*, Kennett Square, Pennsylvania

❖ *Desert Botanical Garden*, Phoenix, Arizona

❖ *San Francisco Botanical Garden*, San Francisco, California

❖ *Portland Japanese Garden*, Portland, Oregon

❖ *Balmoral Castle*, Aberdeenshire, Scotland

❖ *Sissinghurst Gardens*, Kent, England

❖ *Hidcote Manor Garden*, Gloucestershire, England

❖ *Powis Castle Garden*, Welshpool, Wales

❖ *Boboli Gardens*, Florence, Italy

❖ *Villa d'Este*, Tivoli, Italy

❖ *The Butchart Gardens*, British Columbia, Canada

❖ *The Garden of Cosmic Speculation*, Dumfries, Scotland

❖ *Dumbarton Oaks*, Washington, D.C.

Opening to Possibility

"Dare to imagine everything."

—HENRY MILLER

My friend Isabel used to do volunteer work in an old-age home. She would frequently tell me stories about an elderly gentleman who resided there who answered practically every question or suggestion with "No," "I can't," or "That's not possible." No matter what she suggested to him, he told her it either wouldn't work or that he couldn't do it, for one reason or another. It was incredibly frustrating talking to him because, as I'm sure you can imagine, all he did was complain about situations in his life over which he had no control, and in which he was convinced he had absolutely no options. He didn't like the food there, but when Isabel suggested he tell the chef what he might prefer, he would say, "Why bother? He won't be able to make it the way I like it anyway." If it was drafty and she suggested putting on a sweater, he said he couldn't because the only sweater that fit him itched. Clearly, he was bound and determined to stay right where he was, as he was, no matter how limited or unhappy he felt.

This gentleman had completely closed himself off to possibility. Saying "I can't" or "It won't work" was safe and familiar to him;

beyond this barrier lay all sorts of possibilities far too scary for him to imagine. It isn't uncommon to see this dynamic in the elderly, but the surprising thing is how very prevalent this kind of attitude is in people of all ages. It's remarkable to think about, really, considering that the American Dream is all about seeing and seizing the opportunity! It's one thing to have the opportunities and possibilities be out there, but it's something else entirely to be able to conquer one's fear and actually say yes to them.

By opening to possibilities, we can create new solutions, new entities, new thoughts where perhaps before there were none. When we look at a problem and see what might work, we're thinking creatively. When we look at circumstances and situations and begin to brainstorm, we're mentally creating new realities. In these moments, when we inch past the barrier of what is safe and familiar and venture into new territory, we're setting into motion a link effect from one possibility to the next. *No* is a dead-end answer, but *maybe* is the keyhole to new possibilities.

Training ourselves to see what is possible rather than what isn't is the very essence of creativity. Say, for example, you were faced with a question that could have any number of answers. Let's imagine that you're given a difficult task to do at work—something that has never been done before. You have no roadmap or personal experience with this, but you need to figure out a way to make it happen. As you ponder different solutions and ideas, maybe you feel some anxiety or frustration. The dead-end thoughts start:

"This is impossible."

"This isn't my job... I'm not qualified to do this."

"This is ridiculous; I give up."

You start heading down the path of impossibility, sending signals to your brain to continue on in that direction. In that moment, you have a choice: Either you can continue opening those neural pathways that dictate you have no options, or you can halt the process and consciously choose to envision new possibilities. You might not even know what they are yet, but by simply opening to the possibility that there is a solution out there, you're reprogramming your brain toward creative thinking. In this instance, you might hold the question of how to solve the problem loosely in your mind, letting it percolate in your unconscious. Maybe you're walking down the street and pass a billboard that gives you a flash of inspiration, and *bam!*—there is your answer. Brilliant!

The process of designing a garden is really all about opening to possibility—standing before a blank canvas, facing the unfamiliar, and opening your mind to seeing what might be. Cordelia, a quiet, thoughtful young mother of three, told me she wanted to create a peaceful retreat in the area behind her home. She wanted a place to read and to take a breather from the pressures of everyday life. She knew she wanted it to be bucolic and serene, but had absolutely no idea of how to create such a feeling in a flat, barren suburban backyard. For years, she had convinced herself that it couldn't be done:

that the property was too ordinary, the cost too extreme. Finally, the day after her youngest child went off to kindergarten, she must have experienced a tiny opening in her airtight belief that it was not possible, and called me for guidance.

As Cordelia and I walked the property to find the right spot, I told her about my favorite gardener of all time, Vita Sackville-West, who along with her husband, Harold Nicolson, created the legendary garden at Sissinghurst Castle in England. When Vita and Harold first purchased Sissinghurst, it was in ruins, and the surrounding grounds were far from inviting. Though she had no formal training or horticultural experience, through the sheer force of Vita's will and her uncanny ability to see possibility where everyone else saw unfeasibility, she and Harold created what is widely believed to be one of the most extraordinary gardens in all of England. It was Vita who inspired me when I first started out; if she could make such beauty out of those ruins, I could certainly transform a steep slope in my yard into something magnificent.

It was Cordelia, not I, who found a small clearing that would be perfect back in the far left corner of her yard. When Cordelia showed me the pictures she had torn out from magazines (the exercise in Discovering; see page 30), I noticed that quite a few of them contained water—rivers, fountains, and the like. I suggested that perhaps she might put in a small pond, surrounded by a comfortable bench for lounging and a variety of flowering shrubs and trees in the back to offer some privacy.

"But there's no water here!" she said incredulously. "How can we do that?"

"It's very possible," I told her. Digging a pond is not that complicated, and within a few weeks Cordelia had a lovely, secluded pond of her very own. The best part of what I do is seeing the look on clients' faces when something they had always dreamed of but thought impossible comes to fruition before their eyes, and I will never forget the grin on Cordelia's face when the job was completed. Six years later, I still get calls from Cordelia, and each time, I am amazed to see how much further she is venturing out into new territory. Her latest project is the construction of an allée consisting of two rows of linden trees (similar to what Vita and Harold used in the lime walk at Sissinghurst). There is no longer a remnant in her of *It can't be done* in the garden—nor, I would guess, in the greater scope of her life.

Sometimes we need others to remind us that much of what we desire is, in fact, possible; all we need to do is dig down into our courage, embrace the unknown, and invite our creative minds out to play. It is then that we can access our infinite possibility and grow into the fullest expression of who we may yet be.

To try ✤

Ask yourself: *What would I do in my garden if there were no limits on time or money?* ✤

Playing

"I loafe and invite my soul..."

—Walt Whitman

I was at my friend's house for dinner one night when her five-year-old daughter Elizabeth came downstairs, dressed in what looked like a princess costume. She had all kind of beads and baubles dangling from her—she looked sparkly and adorable, and I remarked on how lovely her tiara was.

"You wanna see my tiara collection?" Elizabeth asked excitedly, hopping up and down on little ballerina toes.

"Oh, sweetie, maybe another time," I told her. "Mommy and I are going to spend some time together right now." But you know what? I really wanted to go play with those tiaras! What could be more fun—or more important—than playing dress-up with a five-year-old I adore?

That's what we all want, really: the freedom to be playful and spontaneous, to be able to say *yes* when all grown-up reason dictates that we should say *no* or *not now*. This is one of the main reasons I love gardening. Yes, there is work involved, and yes, it can at times be frustrating when things don't work out the way I had hoped, but then I find myself out on my patio on a late-summer afternoon, the stones warm underneath my bare feet, with a hose in my hand and no shyness whatsoever about spraying the cool water every which way so it streams between my toes and cascades down my back. Indulging these bouts of spontaneity breathes freshness into what I do, and keeps the work from feeling like drudgery.

Being spontaneous immediately breaks through our self-imposed censors and brings us into the unfettered present moment. When I was in my late thirties, I studied improvisational theater with Paul Sills, one of the founders of the first improvisational theater in the country, the Compass (which eventually morphed into Second City Improvisational Theater of Chicago). On the first day of the week-long workshop at Paul's farm in Wisconsin, we played a game called Throwing the Ball. It was as basic as it sounds: All of us stood in a circle and just threw a ball to whomever we wished, spontaneously, without thinking or hesitating. It felt kind of awkward at first, but it soon became clear that if any of us were trying too hard to look cool or be clever, we were missing the point of the exercise, which was to stay present and focused on the moment so that we were ready to receive what was sent our way.

Paul actually learned several of these improv games from his mother, Viola Spolin, who created Spolin's Theater Games. She discovered that these types of games allowed the students in her Young Actor's Company in Hollywood to let go of self-consciousness and enter a realm of total playfulness, spontaneity, and creativity.

Only the adult mind registers self-consciousness; children play naturally, without worrying about whether they look stupid. Believe me, when my four-year-old niece and six-year-old nephew are tearing through the house with me on a breathless hunt for goblins, they aren't worrying if they appear ridiculous. They're just doing it, with no thoughts to hold them back from being themselves. When we can let go and get back to this state, we enter an altered state of sorts in which we are beyond self-criticism. We stop worrying about how we look and sound and just start being who we are.

It is out of spontaneity that sometimes the best ideas and creative solutions arise. I once read an article about an actress from the 1970s who was known for her offbeat and trendsetting fashion sense. Whenever this actress couldn't figure out what to wear, she would just randomly start putting different ensembles together until something caught her eye. She would block out her normal "rules"—*no blue with red, no heels with jeans, no straw hats in the winter*—and just let herself play dress-up with the fun things in her closet. These were the times, she said, that she usually threw together her most innovative and fabulous combinations, many of which ended up starting major fashion trends simply because she wore them.

Play is creativity at work. It's an attitude, a spirit, a point of view, and, most of all, a way of living life. It's a commitment to finding true joy in any act, with little or no concern about the outcome. In its purest, most unadulterated form, play is the expression of who we are when we can let go of who we are trying to be.

Playing is not frivolous—far from it. In fact, one psychological theory states that intolerance of a playful attitude is one of the greatest obstacles to creative problem solving. You can't be creative without being playful; it just doesn't work. Playing is vital to our well-being in so many ways. It increases joy, reduces stress, and, perhaps most important, forces us to put the schedule-minded, results-oriented, and often rigid persona on the shelf so that we can let our unconscious loose and let the true art of who we are come forth. As the cellist and author of *Free Play: Improvisation in Life and Art* Stephen

Nachmanovitch puts it, "For art to appear, we have to take ourselves out of the way."

If you take only one thing from this book, let it be to play in your garden. Play in the dirt, play with ideas, play with new projects, play with possibilities—not just now, in the initial stages, but every single day you are in your garden. Let your mind finger-paint new color combinations, run your hands through the leaves and over the petals, twirl around barefoot under a midnight sky lit with stars. Invite children over to smell the flowers. Let your dog wiggle his back on the dewy morning grass. Allow yourself to get dirty and have fun! In the end, isn't that what gardening is really all about?

To try ✤

This is probably the most loved exercise we do in my workshops; I call it *Playing With Flowers*. Take a trip to your local farmer's market, supermarket, street vendor, or florist. If you can possibly buy locally grown, sustainable flowers, please make the effort to do so. Pick out as many different flowers as your budget allows. Just let your eye go to what it likes and add them to your bunch. Ideally, you want at least three different varieties of flowers, in a range of colors, as well as some greenery and other fillers like berries or branches.

When you get home, remove any excess leaves and trim the bottom of the stalks on the diagonal. It's easiest and most efficient to use a pruner, which you can find moderately priced at any gardening center. Place the flowers in a sink filled with cool water with the bottom of the stems submerged.

Go through your cabinets and take out any kind of vases or containers you have that could hold flowers. Think outside the vase: You can use teakettles, jars, glasses, cachepots, or pitchers. And don't limit yourself in terms of size—even the smallest tumbler or toothpick holder can look lovely holding the top of one blooming rose.

Now comes the fun part. Put on some music you love, turn off your phone, and just let yourself play with different variations of arrangements. Experiment with a variety of combinations and see what you like and dislike. Notice how colors, shapes, and textures of leaves and flower petals work together. If you start one arrangement and don't like it, take it apart and start again. There are no rules here—no boundaries, no goals you need to strive toward. I know there are countless books and articles out there about how to create lovely flower arrangements, but that's not what this is about. You don't have to be a professional florist here; in fact, striving for any kind of perfection negates the whole point. This is about letting yourself go and playing, trusting your eye, and noticing all the interesting things you come up with.

You may find that the critical voices in your head are quick to sabotage:

"I can't do this."

"This is too hard for me. I'm not good at things like this."

"This is stupid. Why am I bothering?"

This is all the product of the ego, rising up to make sure your spirit stays buried, right where the ego likes it, thank you very much. Notice how much you question and censor yourself. Let your kinder inner voice (it's in there somewhere!) lead you through and nudge you into letting go and being in the moment. Remember, you don't have to do this brilliantly. You don't even need to do it well. You just need to do it for the sake of the childlike soul within.

This exercise has so many benefits. It shows you how to start trusting your instincts, allows you to develop an awareness of color, texture, shape, and form (which you'll need later on), forces you to slow down and be in the moment, and opens you up to experimenting and exploring—all essential elements in the process of creating and gardening.

When you're finished with your arrangements, place them in various spots in your home where you'll see them often. Change the water and trim the bottom of the stems every day to continue your interaction with them and keep them fresh. Living with these flower combinations will give you a taste of their beauty in the micro, so you can begin to cultivate your aesthetic appreciation for them in the bigger picture later on. ❀

A FEW IDEAS FOR INSPIRATION

❖ A handful of lilacs in a green mason jar

❖ The tops of red, yellow, and pink gerbera daisies floating in a big, wide pasta bowl

❖ Deep purple delphiniums in a crimson ceramic pitcher

❖ A small grouping of fat, fully bloomed roses in various shades of pink in a silver pencil cup

❖ Multicolored wildflowers in a copper teakettle

❖ Yellow roses with orange snapdragons and red hypericum berries in a brown glazed bean pot

❖ A variety of all-white flowers with lots of silvery greenery in an elegant crystal vase

❖ Pussy willow branches in an urn

❖ Orange Oriental lilies with bright fuschia gladiolus

❖ Fiery red clematis surrounded by dripping white snowdrops

❖ Tall, rich green capsicums, sunflowers, and dark green leaves

❖ Dandelions in a toothpaste tumbler

TO KEEP YOUR
FRESH-CUT FLOWERS ALIVE LONGER

- Cut off one to two inches of stem, on the diagonal, with a pruner or sharp knife under running water.

- Remove any greenery from the stems that will be submerged in the water.

- Use a clean vase that has been washed in hot, soapy water and rinsed well.

- Fill the containers two-thirds to the top with tepid water and add one teaspoon of sugar or one tablespoon of household bleach.

- Keep flowers in a cooler spot, out of direct sunlight, and away from a stove or fireplace.

- Top off or refill the container with fresh water every other day.

- As the week progresses, continue to trim the bottoms of the stems on the diagonal.

Envisioning

Giving Shape to Your Dreams

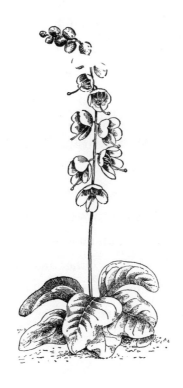

In Stage One, we invited our mind to look within and around us, to go foraging and gather up the berries and flowers of imagination. There is tremendous power in claiming our likes and dislikes, our dreams and yearnings, our aesthetic memories and walkabout observations. They are all fodder for the creative mill. The next step is to sift through these imaginings and begin to organize and prioritize them in order to create a fully fledged vision.

To envision something is to form a picture of it in our mind. Anytime we set out to create anything—a garden, a festive table, or a new employee manual for our company—we must first be able to see in our mind's eye what we are aiming for. A vision is not quite a plan; plans are solid and steady, like roadmaps. Rather, it is an idea that begins to gently come into focus.

Sometimes visions come through immediately, loud and clear. I once met a potter at a crafts fair who told me she experiences fully fledged visions of colorful bowls and mugs, which she then brings to life on her wheel and with glaze. Other times a vision may be hazier, a glimmer of an idea that lurks just beneath the surface, taking its sweet time to gel. Neither way is better or worse—they're just two different creative experiences. Of course, it would be so much easier if all our visions just came to us in instantaneous flashes, but to me, working out a vision is half the fun.

Visions are vitally important in creating not only beautiful works and innovative solutions, but also an authentic, self-directed life. If you can't envision, you're merely going along letting life happen to you. Creativity isn't only about making things prettier or wittier; it's a key element in determining whether you're designing your life, or life is designing you.

In Stage Two, you'll look at what it means to define and own your unique, personal style, to be true to your needs, and to trust your instincts. All of these aspects are integral to creating a vision that reflects *you* and your individual wishes—not only for your garden, but for anything you wish to create in and of your life, as well.

Welcoming Solitude

"Not till we are lost, in other words, not till we have lost the world, do we begin to find ourselves."

—Henry David Thoreau

Solitude is an essential component to creating our own visions, just as it is to the entire creative process. To discover and express what is within us is a solitary pursuit: We may share our experience with others, but ultimately the process happens to and within us alone.

Thoreau's *Walden* has been one of my favorite books ever since I read it in college. Here was a man who dedicated nearly two years of his life to solitude so that he might discover all its secrets, challenges, and rewards. Can you imagine two whole years without the blare of television, cell phones ringing, chatter, or the opinions of others to interfere with your inner process? Sounds like heaven to me!

Many people are afraid of being alone. They keep themselves busy with friends and plans, and even turn on the television when they're alone to keep themselves distracted. Yet it is only when we can be still that we can hear that small voice within. Rollo May put it beautifully when he defined *solitary* as "keeping one's distance from events, maintaining the peace of mind necessary for listening to one's deeper self." Surrounding ourselves with friends and work and activities is all wonderful, but when it's done at the cost of our inner world, our authenticity suffers. It can be so easy to lose ourselves in the bubbling sea of life and float away from our innermost anchors.

For a brief period a few years ago, I worked with a woman named Jo, who brought me in to help her redo the landscaping around her weekend home in Bucks County. I arranged to go there one weekend, to begin the process outlined in this book with Jo, but she could barely concentrate. The phone kept ringing, the dogs were running all over, plus she had three friends staying with her for the weekend who she insisted be part of the process. Every time I asked Jo to tell me what she envisioned, one of the friends would pipe in. "Oh, Jo... you should definitely put in one of those great brick patios... how about rosebushes? Roses are gorgeous!...I have a stone wall outside my house that looks fabulous..." To each suggestion, Jo would nod enthusiastically and say, "Let's do that!" That is, when she wasn't asking me what I thought she should do.

By the end of the first day, I knew I wasn't the right designer for Jo. There are plenty of wonderful designers who could create something lovely for her, but I made a commitment a long time ago that my business was not only about making lovely gardens, but supporting and encouraging lovely gardeners to blossom, as well. Jo was completely unable to sit quietly with her own thoughts, which I found sad. Who knows what brilliance she would have found in there had she been able to step away from the cacophony, be alone, and tune in?

In your quest to create a vision of your garden, I encourage you to seek out solitude as often as you can. Don't ask others what they would do. Don't tell others what you're envisioning to get their take on it. There will be plenty of time and opportunities to invite support later on, but for now, take some time by yourself and simply turn your attention within. Remember, this is about crafting a vision that has meaning and resonance for you, in your heart, and the heart will usually only whisper its secret longings only if you can quiet down enough to receive them.

Of course, being with other people and experiencing all the delights the world has to offer can be enriching, too—I'm not suggesting we all cut ourselves off and become hermits. Yet if we are to really dig down and discover our authentic roots, we will need time to ourselves to do such excavating.

 *To try*

Continue taking daily nature walks, which are a wonderful way to spend some quality time alone. Even twenty minutes a day will make a difference. Visions grow clearer when we give them free run of our quieted minds.... ❧

Owning Your Unique Style

"Follow your inner moonlight;
don't hide the madness."

—ALLEN GINSBERG

We all have our own style. Contrary to what many of the fashion and high-end lifestyle magazines tell us, there is no such thing as having "no style." Style is simply the way a particular person does things. Your style can be bold, elegant, classic, eclectic, romantic, tailored, dramatic, quiet—the list can go on forever. Somehow the word *stylish* has come to be a complimentary adjective—as in "She has so much style." But we all have our own personal sense of style that has absolutely nothing to do with whether or not we have what style doyens refer to as good taste. Our style is simply the fullest expression of our presence in this world.

The artist Robert Dash, who created a spectacular garden at his home in Eastern Long Island, had one of the most unique and extraordinary senses of style I've ever seen. His garden, Madoo Conservancy, is a veritable playground for the eyes, complete with brightly painted whimsical structures and winding pathways that lead to secret delights and enclaves. When I read an article about this inspired gardener and heard how he expressed himself, it was absolutely clear that his garden was an aesthetic extension of who he was at his deepest levels. It was Dash himself who summed this up by saying, "My belief is that a garden, when it is well done, is your autobiography. It is the way you write upon the earth."

So many of us are afraid of owning our unique style—afraid of being thought of as having no taste, or worse, bad taste. But taste is so arbitrary! Who can really say what is appropriate and what isn't? I believe being tasteful only has its place at the dinner table and in conversation, where good manners and tact are generally appreciated. But in our homes, our clothes, our gardens? Why does anyone else have the right to tell us what's appropriate for us?

John, a highly successful securities advisor, hired me to design gardens on his massive new property. He did a pretty good job relaying to me what he wanted: Take down the big ash trees in the middle of the back yard and put in a perimeter of clipped boxwoods, a tasteful fountain and rock garden, and a stone terrace where he could entertain clients. "Of course," he told me with a laugh, "if it was up to me, I'd forget about all that stuff and just build a tree house and a baseball field back there!"

John couldn't see the irony of what he had said. If it was up to him, indeed. Why *wasn't* it up to him? It was his house, his property, and his money. We talked about it a little, and John explained that he frequently brought potential clients in for the weekend to discuss business in a leisurely setting, and that this kind of "wealth-oriented" physical environment was very much in keeping with what they might expect. When I asked if he believed his clients would think any less of him if they saw who he really was, he didn't have an answer. He had never before thought to even ask it of himself.

Acceptance from others is an emotional elixir that most of us crave—and the craving is rooted way down deep. In fact, it is embedded in our genetic coding. Millions of years ago, back in prehistoric times, the only way to survive was by being part of a tribe. We depended on our tribe to share food, resources, shelter, and protection. Outsiders were considered a threat and were usually killed. In a nutshell, nonconformity equaled death. And here we are, millions of years later, living and thriving independently in the twenty-first century, yet that belief still lingers in what Jung called our collective unconscious—the inherited beliefs below the surface of our awareness that all humans share, regardless of our current environments. Though we may consciously know that nonconformity doesn't really equal death, the primordial mammalian brain in our heads still clings to the idea for dear life.

We live in a world that encourages conformity, and for fitting in, we win the prize of acceptance. We're rewarded with praise when we marry appropriate partners, when our homes look neat and our clothes are in fashion. We have been indoctrinated to be "normal" that we've lost sight of what makes us original. Yes, we may fit in with our contemporaries and please our neighbors, but does any of this give us any insight at all into who we really are?

Of course, I'm not perfect, and I, too, sometimes stub my toes against the instinct to fit in. I like things big, bold, abundant, and lush; nondescript, middle-of-the-road landscaping does nothing for me. I know that whenever I plant something small and contained or play it safe, I'm going to be disappointed. Believe me, this is a lesson I've had to learn many times over.

I remember when I first got my wooden chairs for the patio and garden. I bought them raw so I could paint them the bright chartreuse color that I love, but when a gardening friend told me I should paint them a pale reddish pink instead because chartreuse would be too garish, I immediately felt embarrassed by my choice and agreed. Of course, the minute the chairs were done, I knew I'd made a mistake. They looked bland and boring, and totally lacked any essential "Fran-ness." A few days and a few coats of bright chartreuse paint later, they metamorphosed into the whimsical, fabulous chairs I originally envisioned.

I think that in order to live authentically, we need to stop concerning ourselves with what others think of us. We must be willing to live outside of the norm and take risks, rather than risk compromising what is unique and special about us. I know that I don't quite fit in with the typical gardening world, and after many years, I'm at peace with that. My garden is always a little askew because I never quite get around to finishing it. When there's a tour coming, I straighten it up, but other than that I live with a tipped wheelbarrow under the wisteria pergola and half-planted containers strewn about. That's just my style. I have weeds and mistakes. I don't plant according to a strict calendar. I sometimes leave the dead stuff in toward the end of the summer because I like the way it looks juxtaposed against the bloom of new life. I'm always two beats behind, but that's okay, because that's how I garden. If I tried to do it any other way, it would become about something other than expressing my full self, and that just wouldn't work for me.

Your garden can be a wonderful laboratory for you to define and express your unique style. Forget about curb appeal, or what the high priestesses of taste dictate, or what types of gardens are "in" right now. Those may all look lovely, but you're seeking to dig a little deeper! The exercise below is meant to assist you in defining your own personal style.

To try

You'll need the pictures you collected in the Discovering exercise (if you haven't done that exercise yet, circle back and do it first; check out page 30), a large piece of cardboard or other stiff paper (approximately two feet by three feet), and a glue stick.

The gardens I enjoy most are the ones that strongly reflect the character of their creators, be it whimsical, sumptuous, elegant, or mysterious. Creating a garden, at its best, is a very personal endeavor that can be an outer reflection of who you are in your heart and soul.

Gather up all the pictures and start to organize them into categories: one pile for flowers, another for trees, shrubs, and bushes, another for architectural elements, and so on. From there, arrange each pile of pictures on a different spot on your storyboard. I generally like to put the flowers in one corner, the trees in another, the structures in a third corner, and any pathways or walkways I chose in another. In the middle, I put the "mood" pictures—the ones I chose that may not be of gardens at all, but that evoke some kind of mood or feeling that I like, such as a photo of a lone rowboat on a serene lake or a group of laughing people at a wild outdoor party. Be sure to glue the pictures down so you can see each one clearly.

The choices we make generally reflect our style, and when you look at what you've selected, a theme or continuity in your approach will emerge. What is the overall feeling you get from looking at your pictures as a whole? What elements repeat? How would you define the sensibility you see before you? Once your style emerges, claim it!

You'll be using this storyboard throughout your entire designing process as an emotional and visual baseline. Continue to add to it as you like, and feel free to remove any images that you don't want to include. This will be an evolving process as you continue to hone your garden vision. ❧

Your sensibility might be…

- ⚜ Funky
- ⚜ Elegant
- ⚜ Simple
- ⚜ Whimsical
- ⚜ Romantic

- ⚜ Classic
- ⚜ Modern
- ⚜ Old-fashioned
- ⚜ Wild
- ⚜ Minimalist

- ⚜ Exotic
- ⚜ Bold
- ⚜ Charming
- ⚜ Mystical
- ⚜ Serene

…or any combination thereof!

Trusting Your
Instincts

"We must cultivate our garden."

—Voltaire

Way down deep, you know what you like. You know what you're drawn to. You know what will work for you. If you doubt this or, like a good majority of people, feel totally lost when it comes to envisioning what you want, what is missing isn't some superhuman insight; what's missing is very simply trust in yourself.

An *instinct* is defined as "a natural inclination or aptitude." The key word there is *natural*: Our instincts are the most basic impulses formed by our essential nature. When we trust and follow our instincts, we're living authentically. We're making choices that are aligned with *who we are*, for better or for worse. Regardless of how those choices turn out, our lives are still clearer, stronger, and brighter for having listened and obeyed the still small voice within.

Ever since she was eleven years old, my daughter Erika has led two almost completely separate lives: one as a suburban kid outside of Philadelphia, and another with her dad in Tel Aviv, Israel, where he was from. Here she lived a relatively typical American teenage life, but there she felt a deep sense of belonging. Winter vacation of her freshman year at Boston University, she went to Tel Aviv to spend a few weeks with her dad and friends, as she always did—but this time, it was different. This time, the part of her that knew she needed to really try a more permanent life there signaled her loud and clear. It was a tough choice for her, but she followed her instincts and went to live and work in Israel. As her mom, I applauded her courage, but more important, I applauded my daughter's commitment to following her instincts and living in truth.

It is only when we come to doubt our instincts that things start to get confusing. When I was first renovating my garden, I knew I wanted to include a fountain modeled after the Alhambra, an elegant and simple Moorish temple in Spain. I wanted it to be a large focal point at the end of a long, narrow Italian-style allée. The mason I hired to build it kept insisting my scale was too big, and eventually I started to question my initial instinct. Maybe he was right; he was, after all, a pro, so I eventually agreed. Of course, don't you know that it turned out too small? I tasted regret for a long time about this (it was an expensive project), and I really beat myself up for not trusting myself. Now years later, I get pleasure from that fountain for what it is: a reminder of the evolution of my garden, and of my earned self-reliance. It's all a process.

We all have stories about times in our lives when we didn't follow our instincts and lived to regret it. Sometimes we're unsure of ourselves, or embarrassed or scared of where our instincts will lead. We ignore the flashes of intuition because it's easier to let things progress as they are rather than turn everything upside down, but usually those choices never sit quite right. Perhaps you accepted a position that you knew in your heart wasn't right for you or made a large purchase against your better instincts that left you with buyer's remorse.

Maybe, like me, you let someone else talk you into something that was not what you truly wanted. Regret usually happens not when we've made the wrong step, but when we've made the wrong step all the while sensing deep down that it is wrong.

On the other hand, when you make choices that are aligned with your instincts, you build self-confidence. You start to know that you can trust yourself. In the bigger picture, you begin to see that no matter what happens, you can and will navigate yourself through life in a way that's meaningful for you. Your choices will have resonance for you, and in turn you can create a life that truly nourishes you.

Trust what you like, what you're drawn to, and what you sense will work in your garden. If you think it needs something on the left perimeter to balance it, it probably does. If you sense that a wildflower meadow will feel right, it most likely will. If you know that putting in a straight brick walkway will make it too symmetrical for you, don't do it. If you're longing for a gazebo, go for it! What's the worst that can happen? In the worst-case scenario, you'll have something in your garden that represents the creative process you are in right now. You can either fix or camouflage it later, as with my fountain, you'll come to cherish its imperfection. In the best scenario, your instincts were absolutely right, and the rewards will reach much farther than physical beauty.

To try ❁

Spend some time writing down times in your life that you followed your instincts, both in and outside your garden. For instance, here are some examples I've heard from friends and clients:

- ❖ *When I got married out in a field instead of a church.*

- ❖ *When I painted my bedroom yellow.*

- ❖ *The time I bought my velvet couch at an auction.*

- ❖ *When I broke up with my long-term boyfriend because I knew it wasn't right.*

- ❖ *When I picked my dog out of all the dogs at the pound.*

- ❖ *The day I decided to go to school in London.*

Sometimes the results work out as you hope, and sometimes they don't. Either way, the idea is to get to how it felt for you to follow your instincts, regardless of the outcome. ❁

Setting the Tone

"Gardens always mean something else,
man absolutely uses one thing to say another."

—Robert Harrison

My garden has as many different moods as I do. On bright, sunny days, it feels cheerful. On stormy ones it feels turbulent and restless. In autumn, as the leaves deepen to red and gold, it's mellow and wise with change. In the depths of the winter, when all is stark and white and barren, it can feel pensive—even solemn. And when it begins to bloom again in early spring, it is hope everlasting.

Beneath all its moods and faces, however, there is one constant: its tone. No matter how bright or dark or stormy or cold it is, my garden has a very specific feeling that defines it. My garden is, in its authenticity, *bold*. That is me, and that is my garden: In our identities, we are one and the same.

When I was first creating my vision for this garden, I kept making the mistake of scaling back my longings. *Not so big*, I heard the critical voice whisper in my head. *Tone it down...it's too much.* But as I said before, every time I went against my biggest, boldest wishes, I

regretted it. I wanted my garden to be exu-
berant and wild, brimming with scale
and life and sound!

A conversation I have often
with my clients when we're talking
about envisioning is what kind of
feeling they want to bring into their own
gardens. What shall its character be made of? What
overall sensation do they want to evoke when they're in
it? This is what sets the tone of a garden.

Beth, a sculptor, was a spiritual woman who shaped clean, simple
statues. She knew she wanted to create a garden that felt serene,
almost like a sanctuary. When she began to envision the elements she
wanted to incorporate in her garden, I suggested she continually ask
herself: *What do these images evoke?* She asked this question again and
again, and we soon started to see that the majority of things Beth felt
drawn toward were, indeed, very Zen-like: a still pond with fish in it,
cedar pergolas, smooth river stones, a gravel garden, white flowers.
Beth was a natural artist, and her vision grew rapidly; before long, she
had a clear picture in her mind of her future garden. The tone of her
garden would, in fact, be serene, but not because she had wrestled it
to be so. Rather, it was simply a natural extension of the inward feeling she cherished.

Setting a tone is a very subtle concept. If you try too hard to
produce it, it becomes obvious and obtuse. Think about the instant
rooms that are sold in chain stores. The designers, in an effort to
sell "urban sophistication", think of every single detail that would
evoke that setting and work it in—silver-plated trays, glass decant-
ers, library couches, black-and-white photos. Somehow, though, in

its heavy-handed obviousness, the sophisticated tone comes across as contrived.

The art of setting tone is done through nuance and cadence, atmosphere and thoughtful planning. The power is in the seamless details. Restaurants deftly set their tone through lighting—bright for casual, dimmed for elegant or romantic. Teachers set the tone in their classroom through voice timbre and body language. Often the tone of a scene in a movie is set for us without our even knowing it, through music. The effect creates the feeling the director was hoping to evoke in the audience—scary, suspenseful music for taut moments, music with an upbeat tempo for excitement and delight. As a result, our moviegoing event is that much richer. We not only watched the movie, we experienced it.

In the garden, we set the tone by calibrating our plant and structure choices to our internal vision. If you crave a clean-cut, pristine feeling, for instance, perhaps you might incorporate into your vision crisp white box planters, manicured grass, trimmed hedges, tailored brick walkways, and simple color schemes such as blue and white, or all-pink. Just as the choices that appealed to you in the Discovering exercise helped you define your style, here your style helps define your choices. In this way, you create your garden while at the same time fine-tuning your understanding of yourself and your basic nature. It's a dance of sorts between the gardener and the garden, and in my experience the distinctions of who is shaping whom tend to blend and blur as times go by. Everyone and everything grows in the process.

To me, one of the most interesting parts of creating a garden is determining and cultivating its tone. It's all about honing a garden's personality, and once we illuminate this, everything else we do in the garden is about bringing its personality to life. After we know the tone we want to set, we're streamlining our vision, and from there we can choose the elements we want to include out of a greater sense of cohesion and purpose.

*One day when perusing a magazine, I saw a photo of a beautiful country home in France covered with climbing roses. I realized that adding climbing rose bushes would give my new stucco home an aged, romantic look. Unfortunately, since the front was facing north, rose bushes wouldn't receive enough sun to thrive. So I did some research and discovered a climbing hydrangea, **Hydrangea petiolaris**, a vigorous woody climbing vine with beautiful white flowers.*

The first year after I planted four of them, little happened. But the following year, they took off and climbed all the way up to the second story windows, making my home look exactly as I dreamt it would.

*I highly recommend **Hydrangea petiolaris** but beware. Once it takes off, you're going to need to trim it at least a couple of times a year to keep it under control. It's worth the effort for its huge, aromatic white flower heads and glossy green leaves in the spring and the beautiful rust and yellow leaves it boasts way into the fall.*

WHAT TONE DO YOU WANT TO SET
IN YOUR GARDEN?

An ambiance of romance:

Climbing roses on a trellis against a wall…swings and
gazebos…wind chimes…the sound of running water…
a wrought iron pergola dripping with fragrant wisteria…
comfortable, cushioned wicker furniture…tropical draping
vines like passionflower or bougainvillea…aromatic herbs
such as lavender or valerian in abundance…

A sense of whimsy:

A splashy wildflower meadow…interesting color combinations like purple and orange with touches of deep blue or
lime green with burgundy and touches of silver…brightly
painted furniture and pots…patterned pillows…funny
little architectural pieces that aren't meant to be there, like
an old headboard…metal frogs peeking out mischievously
from behind an angel's trumpet…

A rustic air:

Weathered signs…Adirondack chairs…lots of natural
woods… woodland plantings such as azaleas, rhododen-
drons, and witch hazel…random stone pathways…over-
grown grass…

An aura of quiet:

A hammock or gazebo…a solitary bench ensconced in
woodland area of trees…a soft carpet of moss underfoot…
low-wattage lighting to read by…

A modern feeling:

Limestone or concrete walkways and patios…steel statues…
fountains with running water cascading over river stones…
gravel gardens…lots of greenery with minimal color…
straight lines…glass-brick walls…

An atmosphere of sophistication:

Long, straight pathways…Italian-style fountains…graduating stone walls that create levels…neoclassical statues…

A taste of the tropical:

Lush flowers…palm trees…banana plants…humongous
philodendrons…intensely colored furniture…bright
pots…pergolas with sumptuous vines trailing overhead like
a canopy…a tiled fountain…elaborate umbrellas…

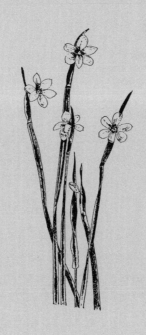

THE FRAGRANCE FACTOR

The scent of the plant material you choose will contribute as much to the tone and feeling of your garden as anything else. Consider incorporating some of the following fragrant plants if you long for a heavenly, aromatic garden:

Shrubs:
- *Buddleia* (Butterfly bush)
- *Syringa* (Lilac bush)
- *Chimonanthus praecox* (Wintersweet)
- *Jasminum* (Jasmine)
- *Itea virginica* (Virginia sweetspire)
- *Gardenia augusta* (Common gardenia)
- *Gardenia thunbergia* (White gardenia)
- *Calycanthus floridus* (Carolina allspice)
- *Rosa* (Roses)
- *Choisya ternata* (Mexican orange blossom)
- *Daphne odora* (Winter Daphne)

Flowers:
- *Narcissus* (Daffodils)
- *Lilium japonicum* (Oriental lilies)
- *Phlox paniculata* (Garden phlox)
- *Phlox divaricata* (Woodland phlox)
- *Violet odorata* (English violet)

- *Valeriana officinalis* (Common valerian, Garden heliotrope)
- *Heliotropium arborescens* (Heliotrope)
- *Paeonia* (Peonies)
- *Crambe cordifolia* (Colewort)
- *Dianthus caryophyllus* (Wild carnation)
- *Galium odoratum* (Sweet woodruff)
- *Nicotiana* (Tobacco plant)
- *Lavandula* (Lavender)

Vines:
- *Wisteria floribunda* (Japanese wisteria)
- *Lonicera x brownii* (Scarlet trumpet honeysuckle)
- *Lonicera periclymenum* (Common honeysuckle, Woodbine)
- *Jasminum officinale* (Poet's jasmine)
- *Mandevilla laxa* (Chilean jasmine)
- *Passiflora* (Passionflower)

Trees:
- *Chionanthus virginicus* (White fringe tree)
- *Prunus Virginiana 'Shubert'* (Canada red chokecherry)
- *Syringa reticulata* (Japanese lilac tree)
- *Prunus padus* (European bird cherry)
- *Pterostyrax hispida* (Epaulette tree)

Planning

Laying Down the Bones

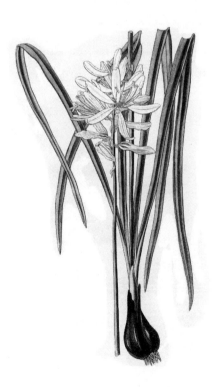

Planning is the problem-solving element of creating. Here is where you will begin to give shape to your imaginings, your style, and your physical reality in order to lay out the blueprint of what you hope to create. You'll take a good look at what it is that you envision and the space you have to work with so that you can create a plan that bridges your dreams and reality, transforming your creative vision into something real and tangible.

I once met a woman who designs and hand-knits the most exquisite baby sweaters and hats. She lives up in Vermont and has built a healthy business for herself, filling orders from all over the world. I asked her once how she designs her pieces.

"It's a real process," she said with a sigh and a smile. "I usually get a vision of what I want to make—that's the easy part. After that, it's days and days of writing the pattern and sketching the design, crumpling it up, and starting over again. I'll move a pocket, change a collar, make things longer or shorter, and basically keep tinkering with it until it looks right. It's a lot of work, but I've learned that if I don't have a good design planned out before I start knitting, I'll waste good yarn 'cause I'll end up ripping it out and starting all over again!"

Isn't that the case with anything we want to create? We wouldn't start a business without a business plan, or build a skyscraper without a working blueprint, or throw a party without having a guest list and food ready. Everything is really just a good idea until we commit it to a plan.

What does planning have to do with creativity? Think about it this way: When you are faced with any kind of dilemma or challenge, the thing that is most required is what is known as *creative thinking*. Remember when your teacher told you to "put on your thinking cap"? What they were really telling you was to be creative—to think innovatively and figure out the best course of action or response. That's what you're doing as you work out a plan: thinking creatively in order to make something where there was nothing before.

This stage is so necessary when it comes to designing a garden, regardless of whether you're laying out the bones of an entire yard or just a small area. A lot of my clients want to get down into the earth right away, but a large part of gardening is planning and dreaming in advance. Without this, you end up overwhelmed and confused, with dirt under your nails and frustration in your heart.

The planning stage of any endeavor can be challenging—it's like a puzzle whose pieces you need to sift through to find the right configuration. I see a lot of anxiety arise for my clients when we actually sit down and start to make things real. But if you have one art form in which you're successful, you have tools in you that you may not even be aware of. If you cook, paint, style your appearance, write, sell, run a business, coach a team, or what have you, then you already know how to make a plan. Draw on this paradigm for inspiration, guidance, and confidence.

A gentleman named Elliot became almost panicked when we began to sketch things out; he swore he just didn't have the sensibility to do this. Elliot was a professional chef, however, so we drew on his culinary creative process for guidance. Whenever he got stuck, we would turn to his process of creating wonderful new dishes and see how he worked it through in that arena. It worked every time. When he was having trouble figuring out where he should put the apple trees he wanted, I asked him how he decided where to put the side dish on the plate. He thought about it for a moment and responded, "I just hold the plate in my hands and feel where the balance is needed." Voila! Elliot already knew how to do one of the steps we will explore in the Planning stage, Listening.

In Stage Three, we'll explore Embracing What Is, Being True to Your Needs, Listening, Experimenting, Living with Ambiguity, and Bringing Your Vision to Life. Each of these is meant to assist you in opening your mind to innovation and mapping out the arrangements that will make your garden a wonderful exercise in creative thinking as well as a thing of balanced, well-planned beauty.

Embracing What Is

"Consult the genius of the place in all."

—ALEXANDER POPE

The irony of seeking to create something new is that you must first embrace the present reality of *what is*. To solve any problem, you always have to fully grasp what you're encountering: the potential and limits of materials you are given. In other words, you need to take a clear look at and accept what is there. A photographer needs to take into account the lighting of the scene she wishes to capture on film; a race-car driver must know just what his car can do and work with the layout of the track when figuring out his course; a pastry chef will need to consider the size and purpose of her cake before decorating it with frosting and flowers.

Meredith, one of my longtime clients, teaches second grade. She once told me about her very first job. Fresh out of graduate school and very eager, she arrived on her first day with a fully prepared curriculum, complete with imaginative spelling and number games. For the first few weeks, things seemed to be going quite poorly; none of the kids were responding to her activities. They would all just stare up at her blankly whenever she asked them what she thought were clever questions. She was understandably discouraged and wondered if she had any business being a teacher at all. Finally, Meredith talked to one of the other teachers and discovered that the activities she had created were *way* above the ability of the children in her class. She quickly adjusted her lessons, and to this day completely appreciates the value of knowing what she has to work with before she starts making plans.

When you take the time to really see what is in front of you, you become aware of the parameters in which you must work. Even though this means you may have to accept some limitations, that's not necessarily a bad thing. Seeing the limits and boundaries that exist move us out of the *if only* myth, which can be one of the most insidious threats to creativity. *If only* keeps us stuck on a merry-go-round of fantasy, out of which we can spin only more fantasy. *If only I had a Ph.D. . . . if only I had more money. . . if only I were thinner. . . if only I had southern exposure. . . .* What good does any of this rueful wishing do? We can either bemoan what we don't have, or we can take a clear-eyed look at what we do have and make something wonderful from it.

Our limits make us into the people we are just as much as our blessings do. My client Mattie is a journalist who often has to work under extreme deadlines. She always wished she had more time to make her articles better, and it wasn't until she was given three months to write an extensive piece—a very generous amount of time—that she realized that time constraints made her a better writer. She drafted three versions of the article over the course of ten weeks, none of which she thought were very good. In the last two weeks, she scrapped the whole thing and went into her highly creative writing mode, cranking out a fabulous piece. She realized that time constraints helped her focus much more, and when she was completely focused, the internal lights were on and the words flowed. The shortness of time that she had always perceived as hamstringing had, in fact, fashioned her into the writer she is today.

Limitations force us to be even more creative. When we're faced with obstacles, we need to figure our way around them—in other words, use our imagination to come up with innovative solutions. My friend Jane remembers the exact moment she experienced herself as a creative thinker. When she was young, she went to a summer camp in the Berkshire Mountains. Every year, this camp would have a playful competition in which all the separate bunks were given a little money to plan out and cook the fancy dinners of their choice (this was very exciting after a long summer of chipped beef and macaroni and cheese, and also not as hoity-toity as it sounds—dinners were cooked over an open pit by the campground). The bunk that created the best meal and table won a big cake for dessert. Someone in Jane's bunk had misbehaved the day before, and the punishment was that the whole bunk would not be given any funds; they had to eat whatever was in the kitchen. While everyone else moped about this, Jane saw an opportunity. Yes, they had peanut butter sandwiches, but she cut them into small hors d'oeuvre-size squares and arranged them artfully on a plate. No, they couldn't buy fancy flowers, but she went out and picked a handful of Queen Anne's lace and dandelions and put them in a paper cup for a centerpiece. This revived the mood of the bunk, who got into the spirit of improvisation with her—and wouldn't you guess that it was this restricted bunk that won the big cake for their originality?

I know another young woman in her early twenties who lives in a tiny apartment in New York City with oddly angled walls and other quirky characteristics that give it charm. She had to use all her creative powers to figure out how to make that tiny space into a home, all on an extremely limited budget. She and a friend built a loft bed to fit in one of the odd-shaped corners, underneath which she created a small meditation area. She found a vintage hope chest at a flea market that tripled as a coffee table, dining table (when she pulled up one of the cushions from her meditation area), and storage unit. Had she simply moved into an ordinary, square-shaped space with no constraints, she wouldn't have had half the fun she did transforming her small space into a multiroomed paradise.

For years, I hated my property. I would look out at the steep slope in my yard and think, *Well, I'll just have to move if I want to create the garden I want.* That slope was my nemesis, but in time it became my greatest teacher. I would not be the gardener I am today if I had been handed a flat, sprawling property and an unlimited budget. No, indeed! I learned everything I know about limits—how they can either imprison or inspire you—from this beautifully flawed piece of land.

In order to make great art, you must see and accept the limitations. Why? Because limits provide boundaries, and the human brain craves boundaries and structure. Take jazz, for example. People think it is free-form, but it's actually one of the most structured forms of music. It always has an end that comes full circle to its beginning. There may be wild improvisations, but at a certain point it is always brought back home. Otherwise it wouldn't be music; it would be noise.

Accepting *what is* frees you up to deal with reality, and to ask the question: W*hat can I do with these limits? How and what can I create around and from them?* In the garden, *embracing what is* means coming to terms with your lot, literally and figuratively. It is so important to consider where you're living, how your land is shaped, the surroundings, and what fits, so that you can create something that's in sync with its environment. The land needs to speak to you; you can in turn create something meaningful out of that.

Before you can begin to design or plant anything, I encourage you to first get a real sense of where you are living, what is there already, and what fits. I can't tell you how many people I've seen rush excitedly to their local gardening center at the first sign of spring, picking flowers and plants at random, without any sense of what they already have or where it will go. The result is usually a cacophonous garden and a very discouraged gardener.

It's quite easy to embrace what's in the context of your garden. I highly recommend the following exercise, which I have every client do when we begin the Planning stage.

To try ❦

Take a walk around your property, observing the shape and slope of it, where it is in relation to your house, where and when it is sunny and shady, the amount and placement of the trees and bushes and flowers that are there. Scan the land from different angles. Look at the outline of the property—is it square, diamond-shaped, or irregular? If you have existing landscaping or already have a garden, include all those elements. Don't judge what you see—just notice it and make a mental note. There will be plenty of time later to register what you like about it and what you don't like; for now, you're just trying to get a sense of what's out there.

When you're satisfied that you have taken it all in, come inside and sit down with your Nature Journal (or a sketchbook, if you would prefer that). Sketch what you remember about your property to the best scale you can. You don't need to have particular artistic skills to do this; you can simply designate certain symbols for certain plant materials. A circle can represent a tree, while a diamond shape might be a bush and squiggly blobs, flowers. Include every detail you can recall and draw it however works best for you.

After you've given it your best effort, go outside with your drawing and look around to see what you didn't remember. Did you draw in the walkway? Did you remember to note the way the side of the yard slopes away from the house? Most people who do this exercise are pretty surprised to realize how many things they didn't notice the first time around. One client completely overlooked a huge rock that jutted up from the ground in his front yard; it had been there for so long that he never even noticed it anymore. Add in what you did not remember so your drawing is complete.

The best time to do this exercise, believe it or not, is January or February. Winter is the ideal season to start thinking about either planning your new garden or how you'll change and improve your existing one. The stillness of the cold air provides the perfect atmosphere for solitary observation and reflection. The bare branches reveal the raw bones of the garden, allowing you to observe how it looks without all the accoutrements of flowers, leaves, and growth. In its essence, what is there? And how can you take what presently exists, respecting the lay of the land itself, and mold it into something that's personally gratifying and reflective of who you are?

The main benefit of this exercise is that it helps you begin to take ownership of your space in a very personal and visceral way. All this is your canvas, and getting an intimate feel for it is crucial in order to paint a personal masterpiece. ❧

Remember to take into account the style and color of your house when creating your vision. These factors will be important when you start to choose plants and other garden structures!

Being True
to Your Needs

*"Plans should be made on the ground
to fit the place, and not the place made to suit
some plan out of a book."*

—William Robinson

Eve was a caterer by profession, and loved to entertain her family and friends in her garden during the warmer months. She always had a particular fondness for a particular area in the back corner of the property, where there was a beautiful natural pond, so she leveled a grassy clearing for her long table and surrounded it by tall grasses, where everyone could sit and dine under the pastel summer sunsets. It was an idyllic setting, but there was one problem: The clearing was forty feet away from the kitchen door, which meant Eve ended up exhausted running the food back and forth from the house.

Eve had made a very common mistake in designing her garden. In rushing to create what she *wanted*, she neglected to ask herself what it was she truly *needed*. Happily, it was easily remedied

Whether you're renovating your landscape or starting from scratch, don't let the cost of the project overwhelm you. Prioritize your needs and just do it step by step as you can. This will simplify the process and remove much of the fear you might experience otherwise.

by placing a resting bench in the clearing and creating a new area much closer to the back door.

Shaping something that reflects your priorities gives your creations relevance in your life. Michelangelo's priority when he painted the *Last Judgment* mural in the Sistine Chapel was to create a permanent vision to inspire the eyes and souls of worshippers. His painting would most likely have been just as breathtaking had he done it out on the plaza in chalk, but the fruits of his labors would have vanished at the first good rainfall.

The outdoor spaces we inhabit need to reflect our lifestyle, just as the interiors of our homes do. If you have kids and/or dogs, chances are you wouldn't want to put in wall-to-wall white carpeting. Likewise, you might prefer not to plant delicate, precisely designed herb gardens in high-traffic areas outside. If you love to cook, it would make sense to have a user-friendly kitchen and, as Eve discovered, a user-friendly outdoor eating area. If you often bring fresh flowers to people when you visit, you might want to have a nice-size cutting garden from which you can pick and choose.

Sometimes it can be confusing to figure out what you need, because what you need today might not be the same as what you will need a month, a year, or ten years from now. Our needs change as we do. A friend of mine who is currently shopping for a home is driving herself nuts trying to see too far into the future: Today she needs four bedrooms to accommodate her high-school-age kids, but will that house be too big when they all go off to college? Right now she doesn't need a formal dining room, because they always eat in the kitchen, but what if one day she decides to start throwing dinner parties? And what if her husband's start-up company takes off and they suddenly have a lot more money... will they regret buying such a small house? It goes on and on, and my poor friend is almost paralyzed with indecision.

I might is no more helpful to us than *if only*. Yes, you eventually might need something different in your garden than you need today. Right now you might need a vegetable garden, but one day you very well might need a wide-open space for kids or grandkids to run around in. Today you might need a place for people to sit, but one day you might need a private enclave in which to escape. Whenever my clients start projecting too far into the future, I gently bring them back to the question: What do you know you need *right now*? Do you know you like to cook with fresh herbs, do you know you have or plan to get a dog, do you know you need to be able to accommodate guests or kids? Anything that is more than a 50 percent probability is worth taking into account; beyond that, you'll just change things as you need to!

What do you need in your garden?

In planning your garden, it is essential to understand the function your garden will have as distinct from its form. Consider the following questions in order to begin to see what your major priorities are for your garden. Write the answers to these questions in your Nature Journal, because they will come into play throughout this entire stage of Planning.

- *What is my lifestyle like?* Is it formal or casual, home-oriented or travel-oriented, easygoing or structured?

- *What do I want to use the space for?* Private time, your kids' enjoyment, entertaining, or simply visual enjoyment from the view of your home?

- *Whom will I invite into my garden?* Clients, family, friends, no one but yourself?

- *What are the most important things for me to have in my garden?* A sandbox for your kids, tall trees for privacy, a cutting garden, fresh fruits, vegetables, herbs, a lawn for autumn football games, a quiet place to read, a space to eat outdoors?

If you have pets or small children, you'll want to be sure to stay away from any plants that bear poisonous flowers or berries, like amaryllis, daphne, wisteria, azalea, jasmine, yew, oleander, castor bean, larkspur, lilies, or monkshood (to name just a few). Be sure to do your homework here!

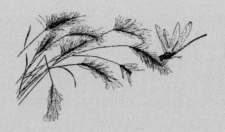

SOME THINGS TO CONSIDER

❖ Do you need privacy from your neighbors? Then perhaps a row of evergreens could go along the perimeter of your property.

❖ If you need to have swings or a play area for your children, you'll probably want them where you can see them from the windows. Take into account the slope of your property when you position them, as well as the sunshade factor. Sunburned kids are not happy kids!

❖ Do you need a shed for your tools? If so, position this someplace either tucked away or incorporated into the overall design.

❖ If you can use fresh vegetables and herbs, you will need to plant these things in a protected spot to safeguard them from hungry neighborhood animals.

❖ If you want a cutting garden or wildflower meadow, you'll need to plant it in a spot where you get full sun.

❖ If you know you don't have a lot of time to dedicate to tending, you may want to consider low-maintenance plants like evergreens, long-blooming shrubs such as hydrangeas, and perennial grasses.

HOW MUCH TENDING
WILL YOU WANT TO DO?

When planning your garden, remember to think about the maintenance factor once it is planted up. If you are looking for low maintenance, you might consider the following plants, which are all quite resilient:

- *Agastache spp.* (Hyssop)

- *Achillea spp.* (Yarrow)

- *Salvia spp.* (Sage)

- *Panicum virgatum* (Switch grass)

- *Nepeta spp.* (Catmint)

- *Caryopteris spp.* (Bluebeard)

- *Lavandula spp.* (Lavender)

- *Echinacea spp.* (Coneflower)

- *Perovskia spp.* (Russian sage)

- *Rudbeckia spp.* (Black-eyed Susan)

- *Sedum spp.* (Stonecrop)

- *Gaillardia spp.* (Blanket flower)

- *Scabiosa spp.* (Pincushion flower)

- *Cranesbill spp.* (Geranium)

Listening

"Wait, listen, obey."

—Rudyard Kipling

In the winter of 1990, when I was formulating my vision and plan for the massive upheaval in my back yard, I used to sit at my kitchen table with a cup of tea in my hand, staring out the back bay windows and dreaming. I would sit there for hours, tea grown cold, mentally picturing what I wanted and where it all might go. At least once a day I would bundle up and go outside on a walkabout, roaming from one corner of the property to the other, letting the land whisper its secrets of balance and proportion, need and calling. It was not until many years later that I was able to define what I was doing all those hours: I was *listening.*

There are times to act, and times to reflect. Times to impose our will and craft, and times to simply step back and listen. Doing and being are compensatory: We need both in order to strike balance. Activity is necessary in order to create our plan, but slowing down and tuning in to the earth and the pulse of the space we are given infuses our garden with an organic sense of rightness.

Every space has a natural rhythm and energy to it. Feng shui, the Chinese system of spatial flow, is all about tapping into the harmonious rhythm of a space and arranging it so the energy flows freely. Really, what it comes down to is one simple question: *Does the space or placement feel right?* Whenever my friend Donna brings home something new for her house, like a chair, she moves it around and around, sitting in it in each new spot and energetically taking in the perspective. I've seen her do this for days until she finds just the right spot for a new treasure.

By picking up on the cadence of your garden, you begin to develop a spatial sense that will guide you and let you feel where to place the elements you want in your garden so it is laid out in a way that is authentic to your personal sense of harmony and balance. This is a subtle practice, very much like being able to intuit how another person is feeling by picking up on the unspoken sensory vibrations.

Bring a comfortable chair out into your garden and just sit for awhile. Let your garden "speak" to you. Take in its moods, shapes, and contours. Where are your eyes drawn? Where are you naturally inclined to want to wander? What does it feel like it needs... balance, privacy, color, more energy, less clutter? Spend as much time as you need doing this (I spent an entire winter!). ❧

Living on a piece of land and becoming intimate with all of its nooks and crannies prior to selecting a site for planting is of great benefit to gardeners at any level, from beginning to advanced.

Experimenting

"All life is an experiment."
—Oliver Wendell Holmes

I am trying an experiment in my garden for next spring. I didn't plan to plant any new bulbs this fall because I have so many other things I need to do, but while looking through one of my catalogs, I came across a picture of the most amazing peach-and-apricot French tulips. They were just stunning. I had visions of a huge bed of those tulips... heaven! On a whim I decided to see what would happen if I planted thousands of these bulbs in my cutting-garden meadow. It might end up being overwhelming, but it might also be interesting to see how it looks. What fun it would be to live with fresh-cut tulips every day next spring!

Experimenting is the embracing of ambiguity in action. The very word *experiment* implies that we don't know the outcome, that we are trying something to determine whether or not it is a success, how it looks, or how it makes us feel, *without making any permanent commitment.* I believe one of the reasons Madonna is still a cultural icon today is that she embodies this spirit of experimentation. She tries on identities like the rest of us try on outfits. One day she's a funky, quasi-trashy blonde, the next a sleek, sophisticated geisha, the next a spirituality-seeking mother of two. Her fans and the media wait eagerly to see what she will try next—the fans to emulate and admire her, the media to usually lambaste her (there are a lot of people who feel threatened by someone who embraces wild changes). Although I don't always like what she does or how she looks, I applaud her spirit of flexibility and adventure. She's not afraid to experiment.

Experimenting keeps your mind limber, literally opening your emotional and cognitive pores. Whenever you try something new, you fire up your neurons in ways you haven't before, and this opens up new pathways. Your memory bank stretches a little wider, and the experience becomes part of you. It's like what happens when a baby tastes new foods. That first bite of peas is unfamiliar, perhaps even a little strange. But once she chews and incorporates the taste of peas into her memory bank, she "owns" the sensory experience of peas. She has grown, just from that tiny bite of round green things. That's how it happens, one bite, one taste, one experience at a time.

When my kids were growing up, I used to tell them over and over that they'd never know how they felt in any given circumstance or doing any particular thing until they tried it. Whatever interest caught their attention, I'd say "Go ahead—check it out!" My daughter sampled cheerleading, rowing, homeschooling, and eventually, living in Israel. My son hoisted vegetables and fruits at a farmer's market, then left high school to do homeschooling and teach basketball to inner-city kids. People used to think I was nuts to encourage them to try whatever called to them and to put it aside when it no longer engaged them; the prevailing wisdom of the time was that I should have been pushing them toward consistency and stability. But you know what? Today these are two very kind, self-directed adults who are passionate about their work and life. They know what works for them, and have few fears about stepping outside their comfort zones.

Really, all of gardening is an experiment. We can think we know how things will turn out and what to expect, but every gardener at some point learns that we're not in charge. The most power we can wield is not over the outcomes, but over our willingness to try new things and let the results unfold.

Before a single bed is dug or a square foot of soil tilled in a garden, there must first be the plan, and there is no better way to work out the schematic of your garden than experimenting. Through experimentation, you can try different ways to bring together what you want, what you need, and what you have to create a plan that works. I love the following exercise in experimenting and still do it to this day every single time I'm designing a garden, whether it's my own or for a client.

To try ✿

I call this the Colorforms Exercise because it's so much like the mix-and-match game of removable stickers my kids used to play with when they were small. Take out the diagram you made of your property in Embracing What Is (see page 89). If you don't have it or don't like the way it turned out, do another one. Remember that it doesn't need to be perfect; it just needs to be a relatively accurate diagram of scale and what is there.

Next, you'll want to make small drawings on a separate piece of paper that symbolize the elements you think you want to have in your garden. Colored dots work wonderfully for flower beds, gray circles for a rock garden, wall, or walkway, upside-down horseshoes for arbors or pergolas, long green rectangles for evergreen hedges. You'll want to cut out these pictures so they're freestanding, like Colorforms.

Affix a small piece of tape to the back of each one, and just start filling these things in on your garden diagram. Play around with them, moving them around at whim and will. What do you sense should go where? Remember to keep your needs in mind as you lay things out.

Continue moving things around and around, trying different configurations: This is the process of laying down the bones of your garden. Focus on the possibilities rather than the limitations. Keep this light—don't get all hung up on making a perfect schematic. Russell Page, one of the most famous garden designers of all time, never made a formal schematic; he drew his diagrams casually on napkins. Remember, nothing is permanent here, so just play freely and see what comes to you.

Feel free *not* to come up with the solution right away. It's not as if you're going to sit down and get it right the first time; that's not what happens. The great composers didn't just sit at the piano and automatically bang out symphony after symphony on the first try. It's a process.

If you come up against some creative blocks here, remember to breathe and to hold the puzzle loosely in your mind. The more pressure you put on yourself to get it right or figure it out, the tighter your creative pathways will constrict. But if you relax with it and let yourself experiment without reservation or pressure, you'll very likely come to something wonderful.

When you've gotten your diagram to a point that you think you like it, hang it up someplace where you'll see it often (I usually hang mine above the kitchen island where I do a lot of my indoor seeding and pruning). Live with it for a bit. Is it working? Why or why not? Does it address your priority needs? Does it make sense? Does it *feel* right? If it doesn't, try again. One of the best ways to discover what works is to see what doesn't work. We all know the famous story of Thomas Edison, who invented the lightbulb only after discovering two thousand ways that it wouldn't work.

Move, change, revise, improvise…this is a puzzle with infinite solutions!

A good garden is one whose pathways easily lead from one place to another and where nothing is placed arbitrarily. As you lay out the foundation of your garden, notice if it flows from one area to another. If the traverses are awkward, blocked, or unnatural, keep playing with the arrangement until it starts to make sense as one cohesive unit.

A FEW STRUCTURE GUIDELINES

❖ Perimeters frame your garden and help create garden "rooms." What frames your garden? Do you need a heavy perimeter, or none at all? Trees, shrubs, fences, stone or stucco walls, tall grasses, and bamboo all make excellent perimeters. .

❖ Walkways are the paths in, out, and through your garden. They delineate the different areas and move you throughout the property, creating the sense of flow and movement. Walkways can be brick, stone, or grass that lead you from one area to the next. Can you easily pass from one area of your garden to another?

❖ What views do you see in your garden? How does the garden look from the street, from your window, from different spots within it?

Living with Ambiguity

"It's not that I'm so smart;
it's just that I stay with problems longer."

—A<small>LBERT</small> E<small>INSTEIN</small>

Planning a garden can be challenging, I know. It is so lovely when all the pieces just fall into place immediately, but how often does that really happen? Usually we have to struggle with ideas and configurations and solutions, constantly arranging and rearranging until we find something that works for us. In our anxiety to solve the problem, we tend to work in haste and try to rush to conclusion, growing frustrated and even more anxious to figure it all out and be done with it. But one of the most crucial elements of any creative personality is the ability to *live with ambiguity*; that is, to be able to sit comfortably in the "not-knowingness" and let things unfold as they will.

In the movie *Shakespeare in Love*, Geoffrey Rush plays a theater producer who tells the fretting writer that things always can and do go wrong while mounting a production. Thus ensues a hilarious road of obstacles and setbacks, each one of which looks for sure to be the doom of the show. With every fresh threat, the writer panics, and Geoffrey Rush calmly assures him it will all work out. "But how?!"

the writer sputters each time. "I don't know. It's a mystery," he replies, shrugging. Somehow, of course, it always does work out. Here, for sure, is a character who has clearly learned to live comfortably with ambiguity!

Have you ever had a problem you were struggling with and had someone tell you, "Just put it out of your mind; the answer will come to you"? Though they may not have known it, they were actually making a sound psychological suggestion. When you're able to let go of the mind, you allow your unconscious to arise and provide you with the answers you're seeking. If you keep struggling, trying desperately to remember or figure it out, you'll hit a dead end. It is only in the moment when you totally let go of trying to think that you're able to see things in newer ways. It is the same when you're trying to remember the name of that person you sat next to last week at a dinner party: If you stop trying to remember, your subconscious will float the answer right to the top and present it to you as plain as day.

If you feel stuck trying to work out your vision and plan, put the "problem" down for awhile and just take a walk—go for a drive—clean out a closet—play music—anything that takes you away from the puzzle at hand. Even if it's hard to tear yourself away, do it anyway. Inspiration comes through the incubation of ideas and images; it can't be forced.

The psychologist Wolfgang Kohler once did an experiment in which he gave a pair of chimps two sticks that when fitted together could reach a banana. At first, the chimps couldn't figure out what to do, trying in vain to reach the banana with only one stick, growing very frustrated. Eventually, they just gave up and played with the two sticks. In this unpressured, relaxed way, one of the chimps figured out how to fit them together and, in a flash of insight, realized he could use this new, longer stick to reach the banana. Suddenly, happy chimps!

When we give up rushing to conclusion and let ourselves relax with a problem, we're much more likely to come up with not just an answer, but a better answer than we would have if we had mentally burned our way through. Whenever Ronnie, a professional song-writer I know, gets stuck on a composition, she puts down her guitar and takes her dog BJ out for a long walk. Usually, within three or four blocks, the answer unfolds in Ronnie's mind. She never knows if it's the fresh air, the break from actively working on the problem, or the infusion of fresh images into her imagination, but it works every time. She has written most of her best stuff while BJ walks along happily sniffing, none the wiser that he is a catalyst for his mistress's breakthrough.

Beyond helping in problem solving, living with ambiguity can also be one of the most valuable spiritual lessons we can learn in life. We live under the illusion that we're in control, but we're not in charge. There will always be things we don't know, situations that we're unsure about, and futures whose certainty can't be known. In today's complex and volatile world, we live with all kinds of looming threats and possibilities that may or may not come to fruition. We can choose to take various steps to make ourselves feel safe and happy, but in the end, peace of mind only comes from fully accepting that we just can't know right now what will be.

You probably won't know right off the bat how and what you want to do in your garden, but working it out is half the fun. Try to use your garden as an opportunity to learn to live with ambiguity. Sit with the not-knowing for a while and see what happens. I think you'll be surprised at how much more inspired you are when you remove the pressure of having to figure it all out and just let yourself meander through it, piece by gentle piece.

Though the genius of Beethoven's symphonies make them seem as though they arose whole and flawless, Beethoven would often go through dozens of different versions before settling on the one that pleased him. He would keep notebooks of phrases and musical passages for years before ever putting them to use in an actual piece. Like any other creative mind, he tinkered, revised, changed, and enhanced his work until it flowed melodiously.

Bringing Your Vision to Life

"Breathe life into your idea and
let it come out of your mind."

—SARK

In every creative process, there comes a moment when the vision must come to life. The first paint stroke, the initial words on the page, the audible notes of a new song: These are physical manifestations of all you have imagined, dreamed, envisioned, and planned in your mind. As Thoreau said, it is fine to build castles in the air, as that is where they should be; the key to success, however, is to then put foundations under them.

It is extremely powerful and energizing to see your creation take shape in front of you. It's like speaking your thoughts: Once you say the words out loud, a sense of ownership takes hold. You have hit the turning point. That which was *within you* is now *out there* for you to view and assess. For the first time, it comes alive in full color and dimension, and the momentum catapults you forward.

Without this step, your creation only exists in your mind. A writer I know goes crazy whenever someone claims that they have an entire book written in their head, if only they had the time to put it on paper. Imagining a book and actually writing one are two different things. Imagining one is private and safe, but writing one means you stand in the face of risk and put your creative work out there for all to see. No one ever won the Pulitzer for a book he had locked up in his mind.

If something doesn't feel right with your garden design, don't proceed just yet. Try to pinpoint what it is that's bothering you. Even if you know almost nothing about garden design, trust your instincts. If it doesn't feel right now, in the planning stage, it won't feel any more right once you plant it up. If you need assistance, ask a knowledgeable friend or qualified professional for their input.

Of all the steps in the creative process, this one takes the most courage. It takes guts to risk feeling exposed and vulnerable, and not only in the face of others, but in the eyes of your internal censors, as well. It is common for people to panic the moment their creations take form. *I didn't know it was going to look like this...this doesn't look right...I have to change this!* The architect Frank Gehry, who designed the Guggenheim Bilbao museum in Spain, confessed that he panicked the moment the magnificent structure was unveiled. All around him people were applauding, and all he could think was, "*My God, what did I do?*"

Why is this stage so fraught with emotional pitfalls? Because it involves commitment: the scariest emotional move we can make as humans. Any choice involves a commitment, even if that commitment is not permanent—where to live, what to eat, whom to marry, how to cut our hair. The paradox of commitment, explains Rollo May, is that we usually still harbor doubts, even once we have committed. We never really feel absolute about anything, and if we do, it's a mind trick we're playing to shield ourselves from the possibility that we really don't know if this is the right choice or not. For how can we ever really know? But as he wisely points out, "Commitment is healthiest when it is not *without* doubt, but in *spite* of doubt."

The exercise you did in Experimenting (see page 103) was metaphorical, and now we move on to the real thing. In the garden, we bring our vision to life by transforming our schematic onto the actual earth we plan to tend. The beautiful thing about this is that you get to try out your plan for real and see if you like it.

To try ✿

For this exercise, you'll need some long bamboo sticks (available at your local garden center), garden hoses, and/or some construction nails and twine (or ordinary string), and any larger objects such as kitchen chairs that you can easily carry.

Using whichever of these tools you feel the most comfortable with, start laying out where your walkways will go, where the perimeters will be (if you are marking them with plants or fences), where the garden beds will be, and their shape. For garden beds with wavy lines, I'd use the garden hoses, because they're bendable and easy to adjust. For straight lines, I'd use the bamboo sticks, and for longer areas like walkways, I would hammer in the nails or stakes every few feet or so and string the twine across. It's as simple as going out to the designated area and beginning to arrange these items in the shapes you think you want. Don't worry too much about measuring in the initial phase; you can fill it in more specifically later. For now, just keep on fiddling with the size and dimension of your plots until you're happy with them.

For larger structures that have some height, such as arbors, pergolas, or fountains, use chairs or whatever else you have around to symbolize their approximate placement. You may have to improvise a little here. Try using three bamboo sticks and tie their tops together, teepee-style. It's important that you get a sense of the scale you want, so try to find or fashion items that are at least somewhat representative of what you want to build.

Just keep observing and adjusting your layout. Don't rush this process. Pretend you are a sculptor, taking in the shape and size of your creation from all angles. Often, once I have the shape I think I want, I'll leave it for a while and go about doing other things, then come back later and look at it again. Sometimes it still looks right to me, and other times I pull everything up and start again. If you can't get the shape or configuration you want at a given time and nothing seems to be working, walk away from it and try again the next day.

At this moment, you will need to put into practice all we've done up until now. Continue observing, opening to possibility, trusting your instincts, listening, experimenting, and living with the ambiguity. All your internal censors will climb out of the woodwork, so remember to counteract the fear with faith—in yourself and in the process.

Once you've made a commitment to whatever configuration feels best, you've got to just go with it, knowing you made the best decision for what you have and where you are right now. Revising and changing are all possible later on, but right now you need to sign off on your present plan in order to move forward.

STAGE FOUR

Planting

Taking Action

It is time to put our plans into action! In the garden, we literally get down on our knees and get our hands dirty—a lovely metaphor for the blood, sweat, and tears that so often go into shaping our creative energy and visions into tangible form.

The stage of taking action is perhaps the one that most robustly unearths our sense of self, because ultimately, *we are what we do.* Our life is not the words we say, the plans we make, or the dreams we imagine. What we say and what we think are all personal expressions, but the choices we make and the actions we take tell the tale of who we truly are. I always say that therapy shouldn't be done sitting in a doctor's office; if you want to get to the essence of someone, get them moving out in the yard and you'll be amazed how quickly the synapses start connecting! It's such a cathartic experience, actually digging, pulling, and weeding—a primal experience of getting to the roots.

There are a few different schools of thought about how important it is or is not to actually do the planting ourselves (as opposed to hiring someone to do it for us). On the one side, you have people like Karel Čapek, author of *The Gardener's Year,* who said that the best way to lay out a little garden is simply to get a gardener. Not all of us have the time to dedicate to our gardens, and if we are gardening with the intent of self-discovery, perhaps simply the design process might be enough to light our creative fires and make some internal connections. On the other side are the die-hard enthusiasts who say that working the land with our own two hands is the whole purpose and promise of gardening—among them Mahatma Gandhi, who once said, "To forget how to dig the earth and to tend the soil is to forget ourselves."

I don't believe this has to be an either–or scenario, though. To me, it's a continuum. Like any teacher–student relationship, the eventual goal is self-reliance, achieved through small steps towards independence taken along the way. Perhaps you do start out hiring others to plant your garden, if that's where you need to begin in order to feel comfortable. Ideally, though, you would do this with an eye towards moving closer into the earth and taking some ownership of your land, perhaps eventually working side by side with others. Then comes the slow transfer of responsibility from them to you. You take over where they left off, like the moment when a parent teaching a child to ride a two-wheel bicycle finally lets go and the child takes that initial wobbly ride herself. You start small and do what you can, learning as you go.

I do believe that there's something exquisitely powerful about taking something in nature and molding it with your own two hands. From the moment you dig up that first clump, you're empowered because you immediately enter into collaboration with nature— and who better to be in collaboration with than the greatest force on earth? The transcendental movement in literature—Emerson, Thoreau, Whitman—is based on our human ability to transcend our self-imposed limits through connection to nature. From the earth we come and to the earth we go, and it is by staying directly connected to this source along the way, that we move into and beyond our potential.

In Stage Four, we'll go through some of the elements involved in Planting: Making Choices, Inviting Support, Taking Risks, Preparing, and Cultivating Patience. Throughout, I encourage you to question where you are on the continuum of taking action, and ask yourself if perhaps you are ready to venture just a little bit farther away from relying on others and closer to taking full ownership of your land, and of yourself.

Making Choices

*"When you only have two pennies
left in the world, buy a loaf of bread with one,
and a lily with the other."*

—CHINESE PROVERB

In one of my workshops, we were talking about the process of choosing the actual plant life for the garden. I had taken the participants through a simplified version of the process in this book, and all eight of these beginning gardeners had created very personal visions of the gardens they wanted. Natalie, a soft-spoken woman in her mid-twenties, spoke up and said she was really stuck at this point. She'd gone into her local gardening center with her vision, her needs, and her plan well etched in her mind, but upon seeing all those rows and rows of unfamiliar specimens, her mind went blank.

"It was like I completely forgot what I was there for!" she said. "When I walked in, I thought I had a pretty good idea of what I wanted, but then there were all these options with all these complicated planting guidelines attached, and I turned around and walked right back out without buying a single thing."

Who among us gardeners, at some point in our gardening lives, hasn't had the same experience as Natalie? The bright lights, the thousands of pretty plants and flowers, the amnesia that comes over us about what we came there to get in the first place? Oh, please... it still happens to me after all these years! For beginners especially, making choices can sometimes feel daunting and downright intimidating.

There is nothing orderly about making choices as to which plants to use in the garden. I could give you a whole chart about which plants you should (and I use that word loosely) choose, but gardening with intent for self-discovery doesn't work that way. That's the well-worn path of gardening-by-numbers. And besides, where would the adventure be in that? Like any slice of life, gardening is a whole world unto itself. The experiential part of slowly peeling back the corner and peeking in, and eventually totally immersing ourselves, fosters a sense of discovery in us. Like intrepid explorers, we set out into this fascinating and totally unfamiliar terrain, armed only with our internal vision and who we are, to carve our own path.

Finding your way through the plethora of choices can really be quite simple. Instead of just looking around and haphazardly picking and choosing, the key is to first be clear on your internal vision, then continually assess each option in consideration to see if it aligns with this vision. This is the formula for making good, personally meaningful choices, in the garden, in any creative endeavor, and in life.

Is this process a bit rigid? Yes, in a way, but any time we are making a choice, a narrowing of focus must happen. With imagining and envisioning, we must widen, while in planning and choosing we taper the parameters as we hone in on specific choices. By continually revisiting your foundation—your personal reasons why—you'll see that within the rigidity of commitment lies the freedom to move forward.

There are two questions to ask yourself about any kind of plant life in order to determine if it will work for your particular garden:

- *Does it fit the tone, vision, and style I want for my garden?*
- *Does it make sense? Is it appropriate for where I want to put it?*

A great example of this formula in action is Marcus, who called in to my gardening radio show to talk about what vegetation he might choose for his garden. His house was modern, and he wisely planned out a garden that would reflect a contemporary feeling: bold yet simple, with clean, elegant lines, a rock garden, and lots of greenery and desert-style plants. The question was, which plants should he choose?

I directed Marcus to check out a few succulent plants that I thought might fit into his vision. He went to the bookstore and got a book on them, and also went to his local arboretum to see some plant life in person. The next week he called back to say that both agave and sedum were the exact feeling he was looking for. He also had come across a photo of yucca plants with their outstanding white flowers, which he had not previously envisioned but got excited about once he saw them in a magazine layout. Because none of us is ever completely singular in our taste, Marcus of course also saw a lot of other plants that he found beautiful, including heirloom roses. But by continually asking himself whether those options fit his internal vision, he was able to appreciate their beauty but not be swayed into picking things at whim. Again and again, he returned to the question, *Does this fit into my vision?*

The second question, *Does it make sense,* basically deals with whether or not this specimen is appropriate for your climate, your sun–shade factor, your zone, and your needs. You can experiment all you want, but ultimately you must have things that can survive in your environment. Just because Marcus might want white yucca flowers doesn't mean they'll bend to his will and thrive on his property. Plants are a lot like kids that way: You can impose your desires and expectations all you want, but in the end their basic natures will determine what they do. Fortunately, Marcus's sunny yard in a warm climate suited yuccas perfectly; thus his choice was "appropriate."

Sometimes, of course, you might fall in love with a plant that ties in with your vision but isn't appropriate for your particular garden. When this happens, instead of giving up entirely on what you loved about the plant, you can seek out a replacement that's similar but will work in your garden. This was the case with Christine, a caller from Southern California who was having trouble with the peony trees she planted in her abundant cottage garden. It made perfect sense, because peonies have a tough time surviving in that climate. I suggested she use native California poppies or old-fashioned roses instead, which would give her the same lush, big-bloom feeling.

In any creative realm, discovery and understanding of the materials needs to happen. Knitters learn the feel and quality of different kinds of yarn and needles, and which are best used for what projects; chefs learn the subtle tastes of different herbs and spices. In the garden, this means continually gathering knowledge and familiarizing yourself with the many varieties of flowers, trees, and shrubs.

My favorite way of learning about plant life is by asking people who are gardeners for their input and suggestions. Call in to radio shows, go to gardening Web sites and chat rooms, join gardening societies, ask friends and local experts—anyone you know who gardens—and I'm quite sure they'll be delighted to help you. The community of gardeners is very supportive and interactive; people united by a common love as primal as this generally want to share their knowledge and bounty. There is a greater feeling among gardeners that we are the stewards of the land, and passing this along feels like a legacy of sorts. I remember when I first started out, a friend directed me to a local woman who sold plants from her yard for $1.50 each. She certainly wasn't getting rich off these precious little jewels; it was simply the practice of sharing them with other aspiring gardeners that gave her pleasure. I think of her every time I'm digging up a plant from my own garden to bring to others, continuing the karmic loop.

FRAN'S BASIC RULES OF THUMB FOR BUYING PLANT MATERIAL

- ✤ Buy plant material only from a reputable place. There should be a planting guide attached to it. If there isn't, unless you're a very experienced gardener, don't buy it!

- ✤ To make sure you're buying healthy plant material, check that the plant looks robust and upright (not wilting) with no roots coming out of the bottom of the container and no brown spots on the leaves.

- ✤ Don't rely solely on what salespeople tell you. Do your research, and read the tags attached to the plant to know what it will need.

- ✤ Save and file your tags. Keep a notebook on what you bought from whom and where you planted it. This will be your future reference in case you need to give it special care, want to transplant it, or simply love how it turns out and want to buy more next year.

Another great place to learn about plant life is online and through books and magazines, where you can see the flora in bloom and read about where they thrive and the level of care they need. You can also go to your local arboretums, where you can view all different specimens in person. There you can touch the leaves and flowers, breathe in their scent, and get a real feel for their scale and their presence. Garden centers are designed to sell, so my suggestion is that you learn your stuff before going. Remember what they say about an educated consumer!

Sometimes a choice will be clear as day, right there in front of you with all the obviousness of a puppy waiting eagerly to be petted. Other times you'll need to noodle around with the different options until you find the right one. If you're anything like me and all the other gardeners I've known and worked with, you'll make some good choices and some lousy ones, and it's all okay. We can make the best choices for us only with what we have at any particular time.

How do you know if a plant choice is ultimately the best one for you at that given time? It is the same in the garden as it is in life: The solution is elegant. Elegance is the goal scientists strive for in making the various pieces of their hypotheses fit together, and what mathematicians find when their theorems unfold seamlessly. It feels clean and appropriate, fitting gracefully into place. This doesn't happen all the time, especially for beginners, for whom the process can be a bit bumpier, but if you commit wholly to this process of making authentic choices, there will be glimmers of it. In the greater scheme of things, a life consisting of many elegant choices is one that ultimately flows forth purely, smooth and easy as a river.

SOME FAVORITE CHOICES FOR
A SHADE GARDEN

- *Digitalis spp.* (Foxglove)

- *Aquilegia spp.* (Columbine)

- *Astilbe spp.* (False spirea)

- *Hosta spp.* (Plantain lily)

- *Dryopteris spp.* (Wood fern)

- *Tiarella spp.* (Foamflower)

- *Heuchera spp.* (Coral bells)

- *Tradescantia spp.* (Spiderwort)

- *Epimedium spp.* (Barrenwort, Bishop's hat)

- *Dicentra spp.* (Bleeding heart)

- *Aruncus dioicus spp.* (Goat's beard)

- *Pulmonaria spp.* (Lungwort)

One of the key ingredients to successful gardening is becoming familiar with your plants' needs before planting them. Visit the plants you are considering in garden centers and arboretums, to learn what they need and to make sure that your plot of land can offer them a hospitable abode.

HOW TO CREATE AN OUTDOOR HAVEN
FOR BUTTERFLIES

Who doesn't love observing these exquisite insects dancing with plants in the garden! You can enjoy their beauty and at the same time aid conservation by attracting them to your garden.

Here are some tips on how to do it:

✥ Use a wide variety of plants native to your region.

✥ Choose flowers with bright colors like pink, orange, yellow, and purple—white also is attractive to pollinators. Don't assume that because a flower is brightly colored that it has pollen. Also, some butterfly species don't see the color red.

✥ Select flowers that are easy to land on with quick access to nectar, those with a single apex or large petals (e.g. panicles and umbels). Good choices are zinnias and daisies.

✥ Use plants with a pungent scent. An aromatic garden will entice butterflies to visit. Some good choices are:

  • *Asclepias tuberosa* (Butterfly milkweed)
  • *Lantana urticoides* (Texas lantana)
  • *Buddleja marrubiifolia* (Woolly butterfly bush)
  • *Monarda didyma* (Scarlet beebalm)
  • *Rudbeckia hirta* (Black-eyed Susan)
  • *Echinacea purpurea* (Eastern purple coneflower)

✥ Plant the garden in a sunny location, ideally with protection from wind and rain.

✥ Place plants that bloom simultaneously together (they're easier to spot, plus more visually pleasing).

✥ Don't use pesticides.

Source: Lady Bird Johnson Wildflower Center (www.wildflower.org)

Inviting Support

"Gardening, reading about gardening,
and writing about gardening are all one;
no one can garden alone."

—ELIZABETH LAWRENCE

The creative process, while basically a solitary one in its germinating phase, does not have to be executed entirely in isolation. Inviting support is often a very helpful piece. From others we can hone our thoughts and learn new ways to expand upon them. Hemingway's works were greatly enhanced by the input of his lifetime confidant and editor, Maxwell Perkins. During his Cubist period, Picasso drew much collaborative support from his friend and fellow artist Georges Braque. Without Braque's input and influence, Picasso's Cubist works might not have had the same depth, nor the same impact on artistic history.

Inviting support isn't about subjugating your instincts or your unique style, but about welcoming in new ideas that can enhance, edit, or embellish yours. I first got the idea for the massive stone retaining walls in my garden from a picture of a Gertrude Jekyll garden in England. I fell in love with the image of flowers dripping down from between the stones, but we have different regulations here than in

England, so I had to build a concrete wall behind the stones, which sealed off contact to the soil. It was my friend Chris Woods who came up with the brilliant idea of inserting pipes in between the stones so I could plant the dripping flowers I so dearly loved. Had I not consulted him, I would have probably just given up the idea of those flowers and made do, but because I did, I live with a breathtaking sight outside my window every single day.

It is important from time to time to hold up our creative ideas to scrutiny to see if they're hardy. Often we can create visions and plans that feel too precious to bring into the light, but if an idea is too fragile to withstand input and feedback, it usually means it has a few holes in it that need to be filled in anyway. Mattie, my client who is a writer, says she always knows it's time to share her working draft with a trusted eye the very moment she starts feeling possessive of it. She gives it to her boyfriend, an editor by profession, and is usually astonished at how much getting an objective opinion and suggestions improves her work. Often he can spot the one jagged piece whose smoothing out can subtly but dramatically shift everything else into place.

When we bring others into our process, there is also a loosening of sorts that happens within. Often, without realizing it, we can hold on to our process so tightly—imagining, sensing, experimenting, planning all in private, without realizing how insular we have become. We get too close to our creation, crowding it and us. Opening the windows to let in some fresh air lets your creation breathe a little and keeps your creative mind fertile.

We can glean so much from others who have come before us. I wouldn't be half the gardener I am today if not for the guidance of Chris Woods and another of my mentors, Jock Christie. From them I learned so much about the art of planting, which is a skill I continue to study and hone every single season. Whether you're an absolute novice or a seasoned gardener, I encourage you to invite support from experts around you. Remember, mastery is not necessarily the goal, and the learning curve when it comes to gardening is endless. You'll simply learn as you go, and ask for input as you need.

For gardeners, continually adding to what they know is an obsession of sorts. Just when you've learned how to till the soil, you'll be itching to know the best way to plant perennials. Once you've learned that, you want to know more about flowering shrubs. Then containers, then transplanting evergreens, then a cutting garden... blissfully, it goes on forever!

To try

Wherever you are in your gardening process—whatever you are working on right now—stop and ask a fellow gardener for their input. Invite some support from someone else, even if you feel you don't need it, and see what happens. Did they see something you missed? Did their input enhance your idea? Did it make you even more sure of the way you'd planned to do it? Is what they had to offer of value to you, and are you open to their guidance? There is much to learn about yourself here: how you take feedback and what happens when you, as a creative mind, open up and let others in.

Taking Risks

"He who plants a tree, plants a hope."

—Thomas Jefferson

Very early on each spring, when I start to look around my garden and envision what I want to plant that year, I always go through the same process of longing for the familiar. Perhaps the roses of last year were particularly fragrant, or the love-lies-bleeding plants especially enticing, and I think, *Ooh, I'll do that again.* But then comes the familiar tug inside that reminds me that my garden is my laboratory for my own growth, and that I grow only when I take risks. That is the tug toward a newer, more unveiled version of myself, and I quickly do an about-face and start thinking about what I can do differently this year.

Whenever we create, we are taking risks. The most inspired creations are born of deep risk—leaps of faith taken by people who dare to venture into new territory, despite their fear, despite the odds, and despite the uncertainty of how it will turn out. In creating Sundance, Robert Redford put everything he had on the line, including his reputation, money, and reserve of energy, to build his vision of a creative laboratory for filmmakers in the mountains of Utah. A lot of people thought he was just plain crazy to launch such an ambitious vision outside of the typical entertainment centers of New York and Los Angeles—not to mention his intent to preserve hundreds of acres of unspoiled land that plenty of other people would have developed for profit. Yet today Sundance has blossomed into a cultural icon, with a yearly film festival that rivals Cannes. The surrounding land remains pristine and undeveloped as far as the eye can see.

Taking any risk impacts us way down deep, in the tectonic plates of our very existence. In order to make something new, we need to relinquish the delicate reality that is right now. To create a new business, we must leave our existing work. To make a house our home, we must take down what is there and create our imprint. To create a child, we must give up some of our independence. In all creative endeavors, we risk the fear of failure in a society that is very success-oriented *(What will happen to me if I fail?)*. We risk not being accepted *(What will people think?)*. We risk giving up the familiar, the comfortable *(What if I don't like the new reality that unfolds?)*. Yet in the face of all this looming threat, we, as artists of life, continue to brave on and take risks, because deep down we know that risks are what pave the path to our healthiest and best selves.

True risks are not arbitrary. I think we take risks based on our deepest desires. Anytime something feels like a risk, we are usually looking into the face of something we dearly want. If we weren't, it wouldn't feel so weighted, nor the choice so infused with emotion. Each time we become aware of these desires and act on them, we get one step closer to our essence. If the results turn out well, fabulous! Our confidence in our instincts grows. If they don't, that's okay, too— we learn something about what doesn't work for us.

Simply trying something new is not necessarily the same as taking a risk. Trying new things out of curiosity is experimenting.

Trying new things *when there is something very real at stake* is taking a risk. Trying a new lasagna recipe is an experiment; trying a new lasagna recipe when you're throwing an important dinner party is a risk. Going out on a date with someone you are mildly interested in is an experiment; getting involved with someone you have intense feelings for is a risk. Experiments are wonderful ways to test the waters and see what you like and what you want, but it is the acts of daring that stretch you.

This isn't about taking risks for the thrill of it, or for the heck of it. That's adrenaline, or counteracting boredom. This is about consciously pushing the boundaries of who you are right now, in order to see who you might become. It's about testing yourself in the face of your fears and finding the grit to move forward in spite of them, giving your dreams a chance to fly, even if you may very well land right on your butt.

A few years ago, I met a young couple at a yoga retreat who were originally from Cambridge, Massachusetts. They both came from respected families; Allison's mother was a professor at Harvard, and Jessie's family was from old Boston money. These two kids were a perfect match: They were both very adventurous, and neither seemed to fit the bill of privilege they were born into. They were generous and relaxed spirits, and were just a delight to be around. It didn't surprise me at all when they told me they had just moved to a small rural town in New Hampshire and were spending their days renovating an old barn they purchased to make it into a home where they could one day raise their future kids. They had created a whole new life for themselves.

What was so fascinating was hearing their story about how this came to pass. They seemed so young and carefree, but one evening, as Allison and I lingered over dessert and tea, she told me about how big a risk it had felt to them to leave behind all the cultural expectations that had been put on them. They went back and forth about this decision for a long time. They desperately wanted to live a rural life, but they were worried about how their families would react, and about whether they would be depriving their future children of an easier life. Ultimately, Alison told me, it was Jessie who said, "If we don't do this, we'll always wonder if we made the right choice. But if we do it, either way, we'll get to find out." And there it was: the clearest reason to take any risk in life.

You've already heard me say that a garden is the most forgiving of mediums, and so it is one of the easiest ways to learn to take risks. My garden contains a lot of risks I've taken over the years, some big, some small. There were the mini-risks, like early on when I pulled out the requisite evergreen bushes that come standard with every suburban front lawn. People from the neighborhood were literally lining up to take them, and I thought, *Yikes... am I really doing this?* It was a little scary, because suddenly I was labeled "different," and because I had no idea what I was going to put in place of those big gaping holes. Destroying an existing reality before the new one appears in its place can be deeply unsettling, but also exhilarating at the same time.

Then there were the big risks, like the six huge robinia trees I ordered. I had seen these gorgeous trees when I was in England, and immediately fell in love with their yellow and green leaves. I had a vision of six of them, arranged in two sets of three on either side of my walkway in triangular configurations. This wasn't something I had seen done anywhere; most trees are planted symmetrically on either side of a pathway. But I really wanted these, and I really wanted that layout, so, after checking with a colleague to make sure I wasn't creating an overgrown patch of trees waiting to happen, I ordered them. Believe me, I was well aware this could look very strange! Once I got them in the ground, the trees grew and took on a life of their own. They look magnificent, and are to this day one of the focal points of my garden.

Every single new planting can be a risk. You spend time, energy, and money. . . all things that have a lot of value. And you never really know how things will turn out. But to me, half the fun is the anticipation of what will be, and how I will grow as a result.

Vita Sackville-West, the legendary Bloomsbury writer and designer of the famed gardens at Sissinghurst Castle in England, never actually thought of herself as a gardener. In fact, she was quite insecure about her lack of horticultural training. Yet despite her self-doubt, she and her husband, Harold Nicolson, created one of the most famous and breathtaking gardens in the world.

Whenever I feel daunted by a new project in my garden, I conjure up the spirit of Vita—that feisty, daring, and often stubborn and difficult woman who managed to turn a crumbling, run-down property into a thing of magnificence, all through the power of her imagination, boldness, and sheer determination.

I have seen so many clients change as a result of taking risks in their gardens. There was Carolyn, a thirty-something firecracker who was so inspired by the rush she got from installing window boxes with her own two hands that she decided to don overalls and paint her living room flaming red, as she'd always wanted. Maybe it was a coincidence, but a few months after my clients Andrew and Robyn pulled down the old, split locust tree in the middle of their yard that had been an obstacle for years and put in the water garden they wanted, they swapped their usual weeklong vacation in Florida for seven days hiking in the rain forest in Costa Rica. Could it have been a coincidence? Sure, but I doubt it. Once you start taking risks and experiencing that kind of growth, it can feel like a miracle—and you just want more!

To try ✿

Think of one risk you've been itching to take in your garden. Don't say *no* to it right now; just sit with the possibility of doing it. That's all you need to do for the moment.

We all have our fears and things that seem too scary, too expensive, or too big to contemplate. But when you're willing to simply open up and live with the fear—not conquer it or hide from it—you're actually neurologically repatterning your mind, easing the path to *maybe*, then perhaps even to *yes*. The boundaries in your brain literally stretch.

By mentally trying on or rehearsing something, it actually becomes part of your wiring. For instance, a skater who mentally goes through her routine over and over in her mind the night before her competition is doing much more than just memorizing it. She is carving the experience of it into her hardwiring, making it a part of her conditioning. This way, when she steps onto the ice the next day, she will know the routine not only physically but viscerally, as well.

> *When laying out and planting your garden,*
> *always go for bold and large rather than small and safe. If*
> *you follow through with this concept, you'll be amazed at*
> *how even the tiniest of gardens turn into a magnificent*
> *place of abundant beauty.*

Preparing

"Tickle the earth with a hoe;
it will laugh a harvest."

—Mary Cantwell

Every gardener has heard the importance of preparing the soil. And of course, I wholeheartedly agree with the prevailing wisdom that if you want a healthy, thriving garden, you must start with rich, healthy soil. It's pretty basic, really. Yet to my mind, there are far more profound reasons to give time and care to prepare your garden before you start to plant.

Conscious preparing yields a kind of intimacy with your creation. It begins to sink into your pores as you touch it with your hands and let it breathe through you. Like a painter who lovingly stretches her canvas and lines up her brushes before she begins to paint, you give yourself and your creation an energetic space to simply *be* together, very much like lovers communing silently in each other's presence. It's here that the intangible flow of give and take, of inspiration and nurturing, begins.

If you rush right into the *doing* stage, you miss out on this opportunity. I once read an article about a novelist who creates entire notebooks for each of her characters long before she writes a single word of her novel. In these notebooks, she writes the personal history of these characters, telling their whole story, even though their background may never be mentioned in the book. She also puts in little treasures and such that she feels represents them. For one particularly dainty character, she attached a small scrap of old lace and a black-and-white photo of an elderly woman she found in an antiques store. By the time she finishes these notebooks and starts work on the novel, it is as if she's simply telling the story of old and familiar friends.

Taking the time to prepare helps us get past impulsivity so we can cultivate a richer foundation. I want to make the distinction between *impulsivity* (which isn't always helpful) and *spontaneity* (which keeps our childlike imaginations thriving). An impulse is an external force, like a sudden wind that blows you sharply in a certain direction. A burst of spontaneity is a natural urge that arises from within. Impulsivity is tinged with urgency and immediacy, and usually feels fleeting and grabby. Spontaneity is more natural and fluid, infused with a calm yet far more powerful sense of action. Often a spontaneous moment is simply an impulse whose meaning and consequences are thought through before being acted upon.

I once had a client named Joel who did everything in fits and starts. He would leave messages on my work voice mail late at night with sudden and grand ideas, and by the time I called him back the next morning, he would have either completely moved past the idea, or he would have already been out in the garden since early that morning putting it into play. I didn't work with Joel very long, because it became clear rather quickly that he didn't really want my input. He wanted to do what he wanted to do, at the moment it came to him, and I ended up spending most of my time filling in the holes he had dug and then abandoned and moving the plants he had placed in spots that wouldn't work. His garden was a mess, and to tell the truth, working with him was exhausting.

The ritual of honest preparation can feel almost sacred. At the beginning of each planting season, I take out all my beloved tools and slowly lay them out on the table, one by one. I dust them off, tighten any hinges or screws that may have come loose, and handle each one. I venture out into the garden and inhale my first breath of the fresh, clean smell of nature. I clear away debris left over from the winter, checking for any damage or signs of new life. I prepare my soil in places that need it, going through the motions as familiar as breathing, lovingly reacquainting myself with the rich, moist, dark earth. It may sound a little silly, but it feels like I'm greeting old friends again after a long winter of separation. We are all coming out of hibernation and starting anew once again.

Don't rush through the preparation stage. It's ripe with opportunity to lay a meaningful foundation, out of which magic can one day grow.

If people would put as much emphasis on the quality of their soil as they do on purchasing insecticides and fungicides, all our gardens would be significantly more healthy and beautiful! A good soil is one that feels crumbly when you smush it between your fingers. If it gets stuck together when you rub it, it consists of too much clay, and you will need to add organic matter.

THE SIX MUST-HAVE GARDENING TOOLS

Trowel:

This small tool is used for digging holes for smaller plants such as perennials and annuals, and for transplanting plants.

Spade:

A spade is usually flat with a rectangular blade. It can be used for many jobs in the garden, including edging, digging holes for plants, trees, and bushes, and digging up perennials for dividing.

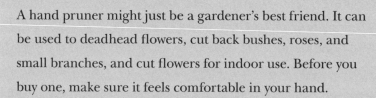

Pruner:

A hand pruner might just be a gardener's best friend. It can be used to deadhead flowers, cut back bushes, roses, and small branches, and cut flowers for indoor use. Before you buy one, make sure it feels comfortable in your hand.

Weeder:

There are weeders, and then there are weeders. A good weeder will be able to get out the root of the weed quickly and efficiently. My favorite one has a slim, long wooden handle and a triangular metal piece at the tip.

Wheelbarrow:

A good sturdy wheelbarrow will make your gardening tasks much easier, because you can use it to transport plants and tools from one part of your garden to another without taking too much of a toll on your back. Make sure to check in advance the dimensions of whatever type you buy so it fits through all your walkways.

Watering Can:

When it comes to watering newly sown seeds, plants, bushes, and containers, nothing compares to an elegant, metal watering can that allows the water to flow out gently. It's a tool you will never be sorry you bought. If you're like me, you might start out with a single can, but you'll eventually discover that it's a real treat to have one in every planting area of you garden.

Cultivating Patience

"I possessed my soul and finally,
though the delay was long, perceived
some appearances of bloom."

—Henry James

Gardening is the quintessential lesson in patience. We learn that we have no choice but to wait for plants to grow in their own sweet time, no matter how much we try to hurry them along. Nature will never allow herself to be rushed to fit our demands.

But cultivating patience isn't an easy thing for us in the modern world. We don't like to wait. We have condensed even the most complex practices into bite-size pieces that are quick and easy to digest. We have fashioned a world of instant mastery in which we can learn languages in a few days and grasp ancient practices like acupressure massage in a weekend workshop. We teach our kids how to play musical instruments in a matter of weeks, then rush them up on stage to perform and receive the reward of applause. In all of this, there is no inner process of cultivating mastery. Yet it is the quiet process—the one that happens in private—that holds personal value and molds our character. Zen practitioners spend whole lifetimes perfecting the art of the tea ceremony, because Eastern philosophy understands that there is always another level. So do seasoned gardeners.

When a lot of my clients start planting their gardens, they rush into *get-it-done* mode. They want everything in the ground quickly, so they can at last see their vision come to fruition. If you're determined to plant your whole garden in a week, you'll probably get it done, but without the thickness or the layers that a good garden dictates. It will be one-dimensional—pretty, but not beautiful, because true beauty must have depth and soul.

I planted my dear friend Helaine's garden a few years ago. When I completed getting the initial plants into the ground, she was disappointed that it didn't look entirely done. I'd put in smokebushes, irises, yarrow, and lots of perennial grasses to give it a very loose and natural feeling, but as with all new plantings, everything looked kind of small and sparse. "Just wait," I said. "Sit with what's there and see how it grows."

Dozens of perennials came up the first year, but there was a lot of rodent damage and we needed to fill in some spots and spray the plants with castor oil (a natural rodent repellent) to prevent future damage, which we did. Helaine was not happy, and I assured her that of course we would do whatever she wanted, but my advice was to keep giving it time. Well, don't you know that in the third year, Helaine couldn't wait to show me how terrific the garden looked. Things were filling out, and the garden started to take on a cohesive shape. It had grown into itself and matured into a breathtaking space. It's kind of like puberty: It just takes time!

So many people want *big* trees and *big* specimens, so their garden can be completed instantaneously, but that just doesn't feel like the natural order of things. If something arrives already finished, you have no chance to ever really bond with it. It would be like adopting a child when they were eighteen: You'd miss out on the entire growing-up process. Remember, gardening is having meaningful involvement with some sort of plant life. The *act of gardening* is very different from *just having a garden.* I could truck in and plant all kinds of great, fully bloomed foliage in your yard, and it would probably look terrific. You might enjoy your garden, but it will never really be *of* you.

When you see your plants grow over the years, you can see the contours of your garden change as it matures. You begin to develop a keen eye for what it needs year by year, and you can add in and change things gradually. You can go on walkabouts: times to simply wander through and lose yourself in the garden through observation. Thickness comes from observing the garden at different times of the day and filling in what is needed to give it life and breadth throughout different moments of sunlight, weather, and moods, not to mention seasons. A garden has to go through a few cycles before it will reveal what else it requires, and it needs a gardener who is willing to give it a chance to grow into itself.

Creating anything with heart takes time. Donna Tartt, the writer who came to sudden and explosive fame with her stunning first novel, *The Secret History,* took an entire decade to complete her second book. In a literary world that demands a book a year for a writer to stay fresh in readers' minds, this was extraordinarily brave. I read an interview with Ms. Tartt in which she explained that it was not writer's block that caused her to take so long; she was, in fact, working away on her new novel all that time. This was simply how much time she felt it needed in order to acquire the necessary luster of truth. She went back through it again and again, adding, revising, observing, and sensing, until she felt it was ready to unveil to the world.

Certainly there are the creative geniuses throughout history like Mozart and Edgar Allen Poe, to whom their creations appeared sudden and whole in their minds, but many of the great minds took years of overlaying thought upon thought, note upon note, vision upon vision. The halls of our great museums and libraries are lined with lifetimes of creative evolution, all requiring a willingness on their creators' parts to see the process through.

A garden planted with patience can, over the years, become a road-map of your life. You will remember when you did this over here, or that over there. It is the stages of your life in full bloom. The memories are all there for you to look over like a well-thumbed scrapbook. Whenever I look at my stone walls, I think back to that highly emotional and tender time in my life when my marriage had ended and I felt like I was literally excavating my authentic self, stone by stone. Under the wisteria-covered pergola is where I took pictures of my kids when they were all dressed up for their proms, and of course there is the electric-blue bench in the back corner of the woods where I wrote the first thoughts for this book. In a perfect world, future generations will have their own experiences here, forever adding to the heritage of this little piece of land.

You can know all the horticultural names of every specimen and talk the talk, but the real criteria of becoming a true gardener is practice, practice, practice. You must get out in the soil and plant, dig, observe, and revise, season after season. This is what makes the difference between a novice and a lifelong, passionate gardener.

FRAN'S GUIDELINES FOR PLANTING

✤ When first starting to put in your garden, begin with the big guys: the hard foundations like patios, pathways, and large structures such as pergolas, and the trees.

✤ Whenever you're unsure about the size or numbers of plants, always go larger and bolder than you originally think.

✤ For small gardens, use no less than three of one specimen. For larger gardens, no less than five.

✤ Work in odd numbers when planting perennials. For whatever the reason, odd numbered configurations please the eye more.

❖ Plant bushes in groups of three or more unless you're using them as an architectural statement. You can also plant several of one specimen dotted throughout the landscape.

❖ Always know what the mature height of any tree will be before you plant it.

❖ Plant in flowing, wavelike lines, not in straight rows (unless in a vegetable garden or potager).

❖ Consider leaf texture, shape, size, and color when deciding which plants to put where. It's best to put different specimens next to each other for contrast. For instance, place stalklike leaves next to round ones, draping flowers next to uprights, deep burgundy leaves next to chartreuse, velvety leaves next to shiny green ones.

❖ Place larger plants at the back of borders and garden beds, smaller plants in front.

❖ Think ahead—try to incorporate different plants that will give your garden four seasons of color and texture. Plan bulbs and early blooming perennials for the spring; summer blooming perennials, annuals and tropicals for the summer; perennial grasses and trees and shrubs with brilliantly colored leaves for the fall; evergreens and bushes with berries for the winter.

❖ Always water your plants before putting them into the ground.

❧ To try

Once you begin planting your garden, visit it at least once a day with the sole purpose of observing it closely. Record every single change you see and feel, every day. Immerse yourself in the details... the color of the leaves as they grow, the stages of the flowers in between bud and full bloom, the tender bark of a young tree growing coarser and braver as it ages. No change is too small; it all matters.

Time won't seem as long, nor the waiting for growth so agonizing when you actually get present to all the little miracles that are happening right now. One day you will come to see how the transformation of your garden, like your life, is really just the culmination of a thousand tiny changes. As you look back, your notes will tell the rich history and evolution of this wonderful place. ❧

Tending

The Act of Nurturing

In Antoine de Saint-Exupéry's classic book *The Little Prince,* there is a lonely fox who is yearning to belong to somebody. So this fox convinces the main character, a little prince, to tame him. When the little prince, who knows nothing of such things, asks what it means to tame something, the lonely fox replies, "It means to establish ties." In time, the little prince does tame the fox, and when these beloved new friends must part, the fox reminds the prince that he is forever responsible for that which he has tamed. The ties, once established, remain intact eternally.

My garden is my little fox. I have "tamed" this small piece of nature. I have watered it and nurtured it and given it my heart, and established ties to this creation. I tend to this garden and think about how I am now responsible for this living, breathing entity. With every flower I prune and every weed I pull, my roots sink deeper and deeper into this place, and like the fox to the little prince, it has become the most unique and precious garden in all the world to me.

It is in the tending stage that gardening distinguishes itself from other art forms. It's an evolving art form, more like the art of parenting, or of relating to an intimate partner rather than to a painting or a song. The connection is dynamic rather than static. Even Claude

Monet treasured his live gardens at Giverny more than his artistic representations of them. A painting may be exquisite, but it will never grow or vary. Water lilies, though, can change daily. When you consciously tend your garden, you reconnect with your creation again and again, perhaps seeing it ever more in new ways.

In his famous gardens at Monticello, Thomas Jefferson planted over 250 species of flowers, trees, vegetables, and herbs. He said on numerous occasions that tending his garden was one of the greatest joys and sources of pride of his life (and this was a man who signed the Declaration of Independence!) Every day he would venture out into his garden and carefully examine every new growth and disappointment, diligently recording it all in what was later to become part of his famous *Garden Book*. It was he who first said, "As the garden grows, so does the gardener."

The essence of tending is nurturing. We don't create a garden and then walk away. It needs us, and through the consistency of presence and caring, we experience our garden in full dimension. I check each day to see if any of the covers of the poppies have broken open to reveal the fiery petals underneath, or if there are any new blooms

on the magnolia tree, or if pesty slugs have been at my hosta again. I believe it is this degree of presence that takes gardening to a deeper level. The ongoing stuff is where all of life really happens, anyway. Parenting isn't just about the high points; it's about the peanut-butter-and jelly sandwiches and skinned knees, laughing as you struggle to pull off wet galoshes and trying not to lose your temper when they tell you they dented the car—*again*. These are the moments we are being real.

In this stage, we will explore Working, Tapping into Flow, Revising, and Accepting. It's my hope that incorporating these elements into your gardening will give you a whole new perspective on how tending your garden can nourish you, the gardener, in return.

Working

"Joyful is the accumulation of good work."
—Buddha

Planting is the big bang of gardening: the infatuation stage, when everything is new and exciting. But as with any good relationship, the ultimate success of the love affair depends on what happens once the fireworks die down and you're faced with the everyday act of relating. The beginning layers are intoxicating, for sure—who doesn't love that delicious, heady feeling of falling in love? The real opportunity for depth and strength, however, lies in the realm of daily tending.

There are times to envision and plan and take action, and quieter times to do caretaking. This smoothes the creative fires into a low but steady flame, instead of having a huge bonfire that quickly consumes you and goes out, leaving you with only cold ashes so you need to start all over to find a new spark. In *The Artist's Way*, Julia Cameron gives her readers a brilliant technique for keeping the fire lit. She encourages readers to do what she calls morning pages, which are three stream-of-consciousness pages they write each morning without fail. Those pages may not be exciting or ever come to any use, but simply the act of keeping the words flowing keeps the creative mechanisms in motion.

In the garden, working keeps you immersed in the process, continuing your sense of ownership and intimacy. Like a parent with a child, you become attuned to its rhythm and its nuances, and begin to just know what it needs. I'll never forget the time I got a call on my radio show from a gentleman in Massachusetts who was so ecstatic because for the first time, he was able to detect the insidious black spots on his roses and treat them (with a solvent of baking soda, water, and dishwashing detergent) without the assistance of a professional. By simply being out there and handling his plants a few times a week, he became familiar with them in a direct and very personal way.

Sometimes tending a garden can feel like work. In fact, a lot of it is work—the pruning, the watering, the fertilizing, and the weeding. There's no denying that some days these chores can feel a little burdensome. Believe me, there are plenty of days in the thick heat of the summer when I would rather be lounging by a pool somewhere. But to me, this garden is like my baby, and I'm responsible for showing up and caring for it every day. There isn't a parent out there who can honestly say that there aren't mornings when she would rather be lounging in bed than getting up to make pancakes at seven o'clock, but she does it anyway. Like my garden, however, the majority of time, these same kids are what give us the deepest joys and greatest sense of accomplishment in life, and we realize that all of this is really just about being present for it all.

Nothing boosts your self-esteem like physical work. My friend Jeffrey used to build decks part-time when he was in his early twenties, a time in his life that he felt unsure of himself and his future. He swears to this day that it was the singular most influential experience of his life. Jeff loved every second of carrying the lumber off the truck, hoisting the boards into place, and driving in the nails with his hammer. "It was the first time in my life I directly saw the results of my labors play out in front of me," he remembers. "By my moving my body, I could make things happen—customers were happy because of something I did. It sounds really small, but I think that was when I first felt like I could have some control over my own life."

With the exception of those few scorching days I mentioned above, I love working in my garden. I love going on my daily walkabout early every morning with a mug of coffee in my hand, strolling through to see what new awakenings have taken place and making a mental list of what needs to be done that day. I enjoy digging in the rich, moist earth, seeing the whole amazing underworld that lives beneath, and stretching way up high on my ladder to affix the climbing roses to the top of the arbor. Most of all, I love the way working in the garden brings me to my own naturalness. I can get all dressed up in fancy clothes and high heels to go out, but to tell the truth, I feel more sensual and attractive when I come in from working in my garden, all dirty and sweaty without a stitch of makeup on and my curls escaping from under my big straw hat. I never feel more like myself than when I am completely engaged in this work and play that I love.

How does true work make you feel?

 *To try*

In your Nature Journal, keep track of what you do in the garden from day to day. Record all the tasks you perform, no matter how big or small. Besides keeping a practical log of what's there and when it was last tended, the act of putting this in writing will likely give you a more tangible sense of accomplishment. Gardening is one of those jobs where you can directly see the fruits of your labors, and seeing these results unfold on the page, as well, will give you a broad sense of the full scope and impact of your work.

COMMON SENSE TIPS FOR WORKING
IN THE GARDEN

✤ Wear a good sunblock and a full-brim hat when you're outside, even if you're only working for a short time. The sun is more devastating than you think.

✤ Set up a pitcher of ice-cold water nearby. On hot summer days, remember to drink frequently.

✤ Bring a cool, wet towel outside with you to wipe off your face and neck.

✤ To protect your back, always bend your knees when you're lifting pots or other heavy things. Kneeling is best for doing chores down low, such as weeding and planting seeds.

✤ Wear long pants and socks to protect yourself from ticks. When you come inside, do a full-body search for ticks. If you find any, soak a cotton ball with rubbing alcohol and apply it to the spot, then remove the tick with tweezers.

✤ Familiarize yourself with what poison ivy looks like so you can avoid it or work well protected in those areas. I usually use Fels-Naptha soap beforehand to help prevent outbreaks. If you do come into contact with poison ivy or other poisonous plants, immediately rinse off the exposed area with the hottest water you can stand.

CARING FOR ROSES

"A rose is a rose is a rose," Gertrude Stein once said, but a rose still needs good care to remain a healthy rose. Roses can be one of the easiest bushes to grow if you follow these tips:

- Plant bushes in an area with direct sunlight (unless it is specifically stated that the rose can withstand partial shade). It should be an open area so that it has plenty of ventilation.

- Plant your roses in fertile, well-drained soil with plenty of organic matter. Although several authorities say that roses can and should be fertilized up to four times a gardening season, I'm lucky if I get around to fertilizing twice, once at the beginning of spring and again right after the first bloom in early June, and my roses are doing just fine.

- Water your roses when needed. If the top three to four inches of soil is dry, it's time to water. Don't water your roses with an overhead sprinkler; only water at the roots with the drip method (pull the hose to the base of the plant and turn on the water ever so gently—you want it barely dripping from the hose).

- Check roses at least three times weekly for any fungus or insects. At the beginning of each season, I spray with neem or Pyola Insecticidal Spray as a preventive measure. If you do find black spots, you can use my homemade remedy: Mix one tablespoon of baking soda with a quarter teaspoon of dishwashing detergent and one gallon of water. Apply this mixture every seven to ten days.

- Practice good gardening hygiene with your roses, removing any crowded or thin canes to improve air circulation, removing any dead leaves, and picking up any plant material off the ground around the plant to prevent fungi.

Tapping into Flow

"Spend the afternoon.
You can't take it with you."

—Annie Dillard

On any given day, I can be out in my garden working—pulling weeds, digging up plantings and moving them around, deadheading flowers, and so on—and before long, I get into that zone where nothing else matters. The sky can fade to dusk and still I can't bear to stop for the day. *Just one more wheelbarrow full. . . a few more weeds. . . oh, look over there, I want to stake those tomatoes before they get any taller. . .* If the sun didn't set, I might just never stop.

What is this bliss we experience when we are so deeply engrossed in our creative process? It's the feeling of *flow*, when we drop our persona and slip into an altered state of consciousness. Maybe you're an athlete and have experienced that moment when your mind, muscles, and will all come into alignment; or maybe you've had moments in your work where you feel "on a roll", so engrossed in a project that you forget to eat. You are still very much aware of what is going on around you (in fact, the awareness is heightened), but you're off in that place where your heart and soul live. In the moments that we forget our conscious selves, we actually recover our authentic selves. Some people call it being in the zone; I call it rapture.

Flow is a psychological state of being in which one moment artfully leads into the next, when all the gates of consciousness open simultaneously in our mind and we can easily travel from question to answer, instinct to action, possibility to actuality. This sense of flow is the high of all highs—the most alluring promise of any creative process. This incredible, undeniable taste of ecstasy is what makes the planning and doing all worthwhile. It sounds like heaven, but it is very real, and if you're working with the intent of awakening, it's very possible.

A woman who lives in my neighborhood is a poet. I asked her about her process one day, and she told me that when she completely immerses herself in her writing, she feels like some kind of celestial magician. The words and images swirl up, and bits and pieces within her imagination start fitting together like the pattern of a quilt. Since she is the mother of two school-age kids, she usually has to stop at some point in the afternoon to pick them up, and she feels a very poignant grief at having to step out of her zone and into the world of carpooling.

This feeling of flow is the best-kept secret of gardening. We gardeners don't need alcohol and we don't need drugs—all we need is an uninterrupted afternoon in our garden to feel giddy and intoxicated. A lot of people in my life comment that I'm always working, but what they don't understand is that for me, this kind of work is a form of playing. Where else would I rather be than in my garden, conducting this beautiful symphony of color, balance, and life?

So how can you get a taste of this tantalizing drug? By relating to your garden with consistency and showing up as often as you can to mindfully observe and respond to your creation. You tap into the flow of a garden by being fully present and completely immersing yourself in the act of tending. You don't create flow; you surrender to it. All you need to do is stay open, be present, and it will happen.

For instance, let's say your garden to-do list for today includes deadheading some salvias, trimming the viburnum bushes, pulling the weeds from your vegetable garden, painting a small terracotta pot burgundy, and general watering. You could just grab your pruner and snip away at the flowers, thinking about what you're going to make for dinner tonight, worry about that thing your boss said while you are trimming the viburnums, slap a few coats of paint on the pot quickly to get it done, and drudge through the weeding and watering that you usually find kind of boring. No flow there, that's for sure.

Or you can choose to slow down and mindfully take a close look into the deep blue faces of the salvias and marvel at the vibrancy of their tender petals. You might squat down to inspect the base of your viburnum bush to see where there is old wood to be thinned out and spend some time pruning the whole bush in places where it has gotten lanky or wild, figuring out how to shape it so it pleases your eye. Instead of just yanking out weeds in your vegetable garden, you might pluck a few ripe tomatoes and taste their salty sweetness. Paint your little pot carefully and with full presence, coating it evenly from every angle. Instead of just sloshing the water around from the hose, carry a watering can to each individual plant and tip the stream to the roots, observing as the soil goes from dry and cakey to dark and moist. The immersion in these details becomes like a meditation, and soon you've forgotten all about dinner and your boss and whatever else you were preoccupied with. It's your garden and you—the full you. The real you. And that, my friends, is how we tap into flow.

Being present allows you to notice things you may not have noticed before, finding new impressions and inspirations. One warm September afternoon, I was in my front yard, kneeling down to pull up some weeds, and I just happened to look up at a particular angle and saw the last vestiges of my deep pink phlox juxtaposed against a wave of grasses browned to a straw color and white roses that had rebloomed, spilling down over an arbor, all set against a brilliant azure autumn sky, and I was suddenly struck with an inspiration. I had been helping a new client design her garden, which was a challenge because the house was a bright blue and we were trying to choose colors that would work well with it, and here it was! We mapped out a garden that would have deep pink phlox, white roses, and soft, pale grasses, and it turned out gorgeous next to the color of the house. If I had been preoccupied, I would have missed that momentary snapshot in time and position.

Sometimes you may not know that you are receiving inspiration for a later time, but all the images seep into your subconscious whether you're actively putting them to use right now or not. There are bits and pieces of gardens I have visited around the world worked into my garden and into the gardens I design, though I can't draw you a specific map of what I gathered from where. It's all just in there, swirling around in the recesses of my mind, waiting for the right moment to come forward. Like a comedian who draws on his life experiences for his material, much of it eventually gets used one day.

Lastly, being actively engaged with your garden is how you get better at your craft. Your garden is your own private university. You can go to school to study botany, geology, agriculture, and architectural design principles, but you'll learn it all right in your garden if you simply pay attention!

To try

Try to remember a time in your life that you experienced this altered state of consciousness. For instance, when I have put this question to clients, responses have included things like skiing down a mountain, listening to music, decorating a cake—one woman even said she gets totally into the rhythm of mopping her floors. Re-creating this memory lets you tap into that sensation, neurologically opening that wiring, so you can more easily have or recognize this experience when it happens in the garden.

Revising

"A true gardener must be brutal—
and imaginative for the future."

—Vita Sackville-West

While my client Marianne and I were planting up her garden together, I noticed she was a little anxious. She kept wondering aloud if she wouldn't have liked the begonias better over on the side, rather than in the middle, or if she was making a mistake planting dahlias instead of zinnias. To allay her worries, I reminded her of one of my favorite gardening truisms: *Planting isn't final!*

I never like to use the word *mistake* when talking about a garden, because nothing we ever do is really a mistake. I believe that we glean value from every single thing we try, especially from the ones that don't quite work out as we'd hoped. Many years ago, when I was first starting out, I planted a rose garden off to the side of my house. I didn't know very much about plants at the time, so I just put it where I thought it would look nice. Unfortunately, that spot got only morning sun, so the roses never really grew well. In hindsight, I know the design was off, because it was disconnected from the rest of the garden; the roses just plunked there in the middle of a stretch of lawn. I have pictures of the garden, and trust me, it was pretty darn awful looking. After two seasons, I ripped it out and moved the roses to the back, where they get plenty of sunshine. But this "mistake" is how I learned much of what I know today about rose gardens. I could have read about what they need in a book, but my understanding is more multifaceted for having experienced it myself.

If you want to grow and learn as a gardener, you have to assume that your garden as you've planted it is a practice run, especially if you're a novice. Expecting perfection immediately would be like hitting a home run the first and every time you go up to bat; it just doesn't happen that way. You'll need to constantly revise your garden, training your eye to see what works and what doesn't, what is needed, and what you might want to experiment with next. The cycle of imagining, envisioning, planning, and planting gets put into play season after season.

By playing in your garden, editing, tinkering with things, and trying new ideas, you're imbibing one of the key elements of creativity: flexibility. According to Phillip Jackson and Samuel Messick, the psychologists who created one of the best-known models of creativity, flexibility allows a person to be open-minded, and to embrace new situations with a sense of adventure rather than fear. When you're open-minded, you can receive new information and embrace problems as challenges rather than as threats—approaching life creatively rather than rigidly. So you see once more how gardening expands you, mentally and emotionally!

I write a gardening column online for a popular women's Web site, and people can write in with questions. I once received a letter from a woman outside Atlanta who had planted a large expanse of all-white flowers in her yard. The garden she'd pictured in her mind was breathtaking, but the one that took shape in reality looked bland. She had thought it was going to be pristine, but instead it felt boring to her. She had tried quite a few different things, including adding new specimens of white flowers and more textural green leaves, and adjusting the scale of different plants, but nothing would make it match the picture in her head. After three seasons of tinkering, she was unsure what to do. On the one hand, she had spent a lot of time and money on this garden, and she didn't want to let go of her fantasy. On the other, this particular garden wasn't really working for her.

I wrote back to her and said that, yes, perhaps she had envisioned a magnificent white garden, but if how it took shape in reality was disappointing to her, what was she holding on to? It was time to revisit her plans and make some bold changes that would give her a garden that would feed her eyes and soul instead of just her fantasy. Maybe she needed to add another color, for contrast, or perhaps she needed to dig it all up and start over. Either way, a radical revision was clearly needed.

Revising doesn't only have to be about editing; it is also about adding new things into your garden every year. Your instincts will change over time, and with each new season, your garden can and should always be reflective of your creative process *at that point*. A mature garden is lots of mini creative processes made visible. Think this is the year you might want to add a border of irises? Or maybe to dig up that old, tired willow shrub and replace it with hydrangea bushes? I say do it! Why not? What are you holding on to?

The key to good revising is to keep revisiting your foundation— your needs, your vision, your style and tone, the possibilities of your property—and to continuously see what fits and what doesn't. For instance, if you've planted a tropical garden with banana plants, palms, hibiscus, and passionflowers, and you think you might want to add some seating areas, you would go back through the exact same process you have done thus far. You would peruse and explore to see what you might want, live with the not-knowing for a while, trust your instincts about what will work, embrace what's there on your property already, invite input from others if you wish, then ask the two telling questions for making authentic choices: *Does this fit in with my vision?* and *Does it make sense?* Perhaps the citrus-colored Adirondack chairs you choose will work beautifully, or perhaps they will not hit your eye exactly right. One day you may even decide that you want something different, like a hammock strung between two trees, and you'll revise your choice once again.

You cannot simply tap your creative nature once and then expect to be done with it. It's a lifelong process: a continual commitment to being open to possibility, trusting your instincts, experimenting, taking risks, and revising. By looping back to all you have done in this book so far, you ensure that your creative roots will remain well nourished.

Adding organic matter to your garden beds is an ongoing endeavor. There is never a bad time of year to add organic matter; do it whenever you have time in order to keep your plant life healthy and thriving.

When pressed for what to plant in late spring or early summer, if you notice a sizable sunny spot at the back of the border, my first thought is sunflowers. They never fail to amaze me. They come in a huge variety of heights, colors, and sizes. All you have to do is closely follow the directions on the back of the pack and let those wispy, narrow seeds work their magic.

TIPS FOR CONTAINER GARDENING

❖ If you're not using a new container, wash out the old one with warm sudsy water and a splash of bleach.

❖ Make sure the container has drainage holes and a saucer (with a lip) underneath to catch excess water.

❖ Cover the drainage holes with either shards of a broken clay pot or a small section of window screen. Partially covering the holes in this way prevents the water from gushing out the bottom. Do not plug the holes entirely.

❖ Fill the container two-thirds full with soilless potting mix (for indoor plants especially) or a fine-quality potting soil. There are many good brand names. Try to find one that has a slow-release fertilizer already added to it.

❖ Add water-retaining gel crystals to potting soil (the amount depends on the size of container; the back label will specify).

❖ Take the plant out of its existing container. Tip the container on its side and gently squeeze the plant and its roots out (especially if it's plastic). Make sure, regardless of the method you choose, that you don't pull the plant out by yanking on its stem. Remember, the roots of the plant need to remain intact.

- ❖ Remove any dead or scraggly leaves.

- ❖ Position the plant at the same level as it was in the previous pot, making sure that it's nestled into its new home, adding more soil as needed.

- ❖ Leave enough space between the soil and the top of the pot so that you can water the plant comfortably without water spilling over the edges.

- ❖ Water your newly planted specimen.

NATURAL PEST CONTROL

Don't use toxic chemicals to deter pests from your garden. Often, natural remedies are the best. Some of my favorites:

❖ To trap slugs, cut a yogurt, cottage cheese, or butter container down to two inches high and fill it with beer. Place the container near the plants that seem to attract slugs—they will by nature climb in for a nip of brew.

❖ To repel Japanese beetles and other insects such as caterpillars, mealybugs, and bagworms, use neem oil. It keeps away the pests without harming beneficial insects like ladybugs or whiteflies.

❖ To keep groundhogs away, use fencing four to five feet high that's also buried at least eighteen inches underground. Also, hot-pepper spray has proven to be frequently effective.

❖ To chase away moles (my personal nemesis!), purchase mole-chaser windmill-like fans and/or mole and gopher repellent (made of castor oil). Moles are frequently attracted to certain areas because they are going after grubs and earthworms, so if you have moles, check your lawn to make sure that grubs are not a problem.

❖ If you have cats coming around doing damage, lay down rough-textured mulch or large stones to repel them. I like to lay down chicken wire on the soil and cover it with mulch—this seems to keep them out of my garden beds. Also, cats do not like the smell of anise oil, so you can spray it around liberally.

✤ To keep deer away, cut a bar of Irish Spring soap into chunks and place them in an old pair of nylon panty-hose (you can cut the hose about ten inches from the toe and just use the bottom portion). Hang these from deer-prone bushes and trees at waist level, spacing them twenty-five feet apart. Other remedies include Liquid Fence spray, electric deer repellents, Deer Off, and Garlic Clips. Certain plants such as lemon thyme, spear-mint, lamb's ears, and rosemary also deter deer.

✤ If ants are a problem, saturate cotton balls with pepper-mint oil and place where needed for an old-fashioned but effective remedy.

Accepting

"Wherever humans garden magnificently,
there are magnificent heartbreaks."

—HENRY MITCHELL

A garden can enhance your life, but yes, a garden can indeed also break your heart. There isn't a gardener alive who has not been devastated by an early killing frost, or watched with dismay the demise of a beloved plant at the hands of little pests, or been bitterly disappointed because a tree withered and died for no apparent reason. Acceptance is a big part of the game, because ultimately, we are not in charge.

Much as we like to think we control everything, we don't. There is a force much greater than us out there. Nature, God, call it whatever you like, but it's there. We can do everything right—secure an appropriate, healthy plant in good soil, fertilize it, tend it—and still it might not survive. Sometimes there is no rhyme or reason to why things don't work in the garden, and we must expand ourselves even more to accept this.

There is nothing smooth about the creative process, either. We're like ships out at sea: Sometimes the sailing is smooth, and sometimes we get caught in a storm and all we can do is ride it out.

And sometimes we even capsize and have to right ourselves all over again. It's always a risk just to leave the shore, but none of us embraces a creative life because we crave safety. No, it's the exhilaration of venturing out and of putting all we are on the line to see what comes of it, that makes living an authentic, creative life so fulfilling.

In her book *If Life Is a Game, These are the Rules*, Cherie Carter-Scott defines acceptance as "the act of embracing what life presents to you with a good attitude." Attitude is the key element here, and I absolutely believe that gardening gives a great opportunity to foster a positive perspective. As a breed, we gardeners tend to be optimistic, and this isn't by accident. We plant seeds and bulbs with the faith that they will, in fact, grow. Is there anything more hopeful or positive than the first appearance of bloom? There is something very encouraging about bearing direct witness to the cycles of birth, death, and renewal all playing out right there in front of our eyes. Yes, it is disappointing when something we worked hard to nurture doesn't survive, but there is always another specimen to try, another bulb to embed.

A local gardening friend of mine had an enormous pine tree in his front yard that was struck by lightning in a violent summer storm. The tree splintered, and half of it came crashing down. Luckily it fell away from the house, so there was no damage and no one was hurt, but the tree was so badly damaged that it had to be cut down entirely. I went over to keep him company as professional arborists pulled the mighty roots of this stump out of the ground. When they were done, there was a huge gaping hole in his lawn.

"Shame about that tree," one of the guys said. "And now you've got this big mess of a hole here."

My friend, a lifelong gardener, just smiled and quietly said to me, "True, but think of all the new things I can plant here now!"

Sometimes your creative endeavors won't work out as you had planned; that's a fact of life. Maybe your artwork won't sell, or maybe the business you started won't get off the ground. What matters is that you simply view these letdowns as part of the process and just keep on going. Acceptance is very simply the art of repeatedly *embracing what is,* no matter what. As we already know, holding on to what was or what might have been is a trap that keeps us stuck, but acceptance gives us peace of mind in the present, so we are free to continue creating in the future.

GET RID OF THE GRASS AND REPLACE WITH NATIVE PLANTS!

Native plants offer the following benefits:

- ⚜ Reduce water needs.

- ⚜ Provide a landscape that can prosper despite temperature fluctuations.

- ⚜ Minimize the amount of pesticides and fertilizer needed.

- ⚜ Prevent the potential of an eyesore when reduced rainfall causes water shortages that turn lawns brown.

- ⚜ Locally native plants are wildlife-friendly and provide the best overall food sources for backyard birds and other animals. They may support ten to fifty times as many species of wildlife as non-native plants.

Source: National Wildlife Federation (www.nwf.org)

SQUEEZED FOR TIME
BUT WANT TO GARDEN?

Like a workout, run, or practicing a musical instrument, you can get a lot done in the garden doing it in short and concentrated chunks of time.

Here's how with *Gardening in Thirty Minutes*.

❖ When it comes to doing short spurts of gardening, if you put your mind to it, you'll be able to complete some significant gardening tasks in only half an hour.

❖ Make a list of what you'd like to accomplish in the garden for the coming week, prioritizing your list so that the most important chores are at the top.

❖ Break up some of the larger jobs into smaller, manageable tasks. For example, if you have three separate garden beds that need weeding, select one of the beds and begin with it. At your next thirty-minute session, pick up with where you left off. The same process can be followed for other gardening jobs.

❖ Practice *mindful gardening.* This means totally focusing on the task at hand without any interruptions. When your mind begins to wander, gently but firmly lead it back to what you're doing. It may feel a bit forced at first, but once you get the hang of it, you'll look forward to your thirty-minute gardening sessions as much for the calming rejuvenation that you'll experience as the gradual and methodical way your garden tasks will get completed.

Enjoying

Reaping What You Have Sown

Over the years, I've been privileged to hear so many great stories about people's experiences in their gardens. There are few things in life that can touch us the way nature can, and fewer still that combine the awesome power of nature and the intense satisfaction of creating something with our own hands. These tiny corners of earth that we call our own can provide us with so very much more than just pretty flowers and a comfortable place to sit.

There is the story of Samantha and Michael who tend a small apple orchard on their farm in western New Jersey. Every year in early autumn, they throw a big party for all the local kids, filled with apple picking, bobbing for apples, pumpkin carving, and other fun activities. Or the story of Janet, who called my radio show to ask how she could transplant the Japanese maple from her sister's yard to her own. Her sister had recently passed away, and Janet wanted that tree close to her so she could feel her sister's presence. Or Ruth, who quietly slips outside into her garden to sit on her painted bench and find the moon at night, long after her family has gone to bed. For all of these people, and so many others, a garden is a chance to pause and simply relish *being*.

Enjoyment of your garden can provide you with a myriad of gifts. A garden can be a retreat that nourishes your spirit, like the exquisite

Zen garden and meditation chapel at the Omega Institute for Holistic Studies in upstate New York. There is something almost holy about the tranquility of that space that makes my soul feel infinite. A garden can heal, like the ones created in hospitals around the country to give hope or solace to patients and their families. A garden can be like a dear friend, who inspires, guides, mirrors your process, or is simply there through thick and thin. My own garden is there to support me through all the ups and downs of my life. It soothes me when I'm worried about Erika or Jason, celebrates with me when something wonderful happens, and helps me heal during times of great pain. Whenever I want to get to myself and my feelings, my garden facilitates that.

In this stage, we'll explore what it means to truly appreciate your creations and how both you and those around you are enriched by your sharing your creation with the world.

Appreciating

"I have, as it were, my own sun and moon and stars, and a little world all to myself."

—HENRY DAVID THOREAU

One evening in midsummer, I was sitting out in my garden with my friend Glynnis, having a glass of wine and catching up. At some point Glynnis looked around and asked me, "Don't you ever get lonely here?"

"Sure, sometimes I wish my kids were back home," I admitted. Of course I miss the rattle and hum of family life. But then I look around my garden and watch the squirrels making their frantic dashes, the lusty bees crazily searching for one more flower to pollinate, and the soft boughs of the evergreen trees swaying gently in the breeze... and I think, *How could I ever be lonely with all of this?*

It's funny, I know, but sometimes I feel like the Dr. Doolittle of gardening. I have brought (or lured) all these plants and animals here to coexist and do what they do, and they are all welcome. Opening my home and my life to such extraordinary dances of nature and balance makes me feel content deep down in my bones. It makes me appreciate my garden and my life on a whole other level.

There are so many different facets to appreciating a garden: giving thanks for its presence, valuing what it provides, delighting in its beauty, understanding all that it represents and encompasses. As we do these things, our roots implant deeper into the soul of the place, and as the creator, we are able to draw sustenance from our creation.

It is with a sense of awe and gratitude that I walk through my garden on my early-morning walkabouts. The sights, the scents, the sounds, and the air impart a sense of grace that makes everything feel as though it is right where it should be. In these moments, I know just what Elizabeth Barrett Browning meant when she wrote, "Earth's crammed with heaven, and every common bush afire with God."

Savoring your garden brings more than just sensory pleasure, though; it fills your creative well. In the moments that you experience the reverie of simply being there without working or planning or doing anything other than just drinking it in, you can experience a heightened awareness that elevates your consciousness. Any expression of art, be it a Rembrandt or your own garden, reflects the best of humankind, and tapping into this wonder expands your creative capacity so you can in turn create even more art—more awareness—more inspiration—more aliveness. The cycle feeds itself, but only if you stop to smell those literal and proverbial roses.

An appreciation for beauty is not frivolous. It is very real, and very valuable. Howard Gardner, a psychologist at Harvard University, is doing a lot of good research on "aesthetic intelligence," a character trait that gives us a greater capacity or need for beauty, much the way linear intelligence can make us proficient in numbers.

Immersing yourself in beauty can have a profound effect on how you live. Years ago, I started a program bringing inner-city kids to Chanticleer Gardens so they could glimpse a slice of nature they were not normally exposed to. You should have seen the looks on these kids' faces when they saw the gardens! It was as if I'd opened the gates to Disneyland. Chris Woods, who at that time ran Chanticleer, let them wander around and roll down a huge hill of perfectly manicured grass—they were ecstatic! Beyond the freedom and fun they tasted that day, I knew this kind of exposure would open up vistas in their imaginations. Five or six years later, many of these kids still called me to talk about how profound that experience was for them. I lost track of them as the years went by, but I like to think that their lives today contain an amplified appreciation of beauty and what they themselves are capable of.

Beauty feeds our creative natures by giving us inspiration and aspiration. When I was young and used to go see modern dance performances, I was so moved by what these bodies could do. I left the theater feeling more hopeful, yearning to reach into my own potential. What happens is like a quiet mentoring: The beauty creator inspires the beauty appreciators, who in turn become their own beauty creators and go on to inspire others. This is why beauty is so essential in the life of a creative spirit.

I do know people who claim they don't have the time or inclination to pause and enjoy their gardens. A lot of goal-oriented personalities look around their gardens and only see the weeds that need to be pulled—everything they need to do, master, conquer. Yet I believe that if we don't pause and relish the work we've done, we simply swing from task to task and forget to do all those things we did in Stage One that feed our imagination, such as observing, discovering, exploring, and playing. Appreciation of our past creative efforts is like fuel for the future ones.

When Wendy, a gifted landscape architect I work with from time to time, is in the early days of starting a new project, she frequently goes back to visit properties she designed in the past. In the initial moments of imagining and envisioning her new project, she looks back at her past accomplishments to boost her confidence. After getting some distance from these works, she's often surprised when she looks at them with fresh eyes at how good a job she actually did! She's reminded to trust her instincts, own her unique style, and be true to the needs and reality of the new space. When she reaches the planning/problem-solving stage in her new project, seeing her other completed works helps her live with the ambiguity, reminding her that she has found her way through complex puzzles in the past, usually to beautiful results.

By nature, human beings are task-oriented, but we also need to feel the rewards of our hard work to assimilate into our psyche the scope and meaning of what we have done. This happens in yoga practice; after doing however many minutes of postures and breathing, you lie still in Savasana (corpse pose) so your nervous system can integrate the energy you've moved and the conduits you've reprogrammed. You wouldn't reap the same benefits if you just did your poses and leapt up off your mat and out into your day.

It's the same for the creative process. A lot of internal shifts happen when you're creating, and you need reflective time to absorb the impact of these shifts if the process is to have any lasting effect. Carla, who faithfully works in her garden every Saturday and Sunday, always makes sure she leaves at least fifteen minutes at the end of every workday to sit back and take in what she has done. Sometimes she feels pride, sometimes gratitude that the workday is done, sometimes a deep sense of accomplishment; other times she just sits and soaks up the beauty around her.

Your appreciation of things is uniquely yours. Any moment you experience a sense of reverie, you're aligning with your true nature and what makes your private heart sing. To experience sensation on all five cylinders is to be profoundly *alive*, existentially joyful and present to our authentic self in the context of our unique and astonishing journey here.

 ## To try

As often as you can, follow Carla's lead and spend a few moments in your garden, preferably in the early morning or at the end of the day, doing nothing but taking it in. Write down in your Nature Journal at least one thing in your garden that you appreciate: a visual detail, the way something made you feel, or just the fact that it's there today to envelop you. I do this exercise often, and usually find far more than one thing that gave me joy that day.

THE PLEASURE OF FRESH-CUT FLOWERS

Morning is the best time to cut fresh flowers from the garden, before the heat of the day hits and wilts them slightly. When you cut multiple-stem flowers, like yarrows or daisies, choose those that have at least one bud that's opening and another that's almost ready to open. Flowers that grow on individual stems, such as roses or phlox, should be cut when they're already open.

If you're concerned that cutting fresh flowers from the garden will leave your garden looking sparse, well, fear no more. The cutting of the flowers actually encourages more flowering and growth on the plants, similar to deadheading. I like to think of this as nature's way of encouraging us to appreciate and share her bounty!

HOMEGROWN DELIGHTS

The writer Lewis Grizzard once said, "It is difficult to think about anything but pleasant thoughts while eating a homegrown tomato." How right he is! Enjoying food you grow with your own two hands is as basic and primordial as humankind itself. If you have the space for it, I encourage you to plant even a few vegetables in your garden. Tomatoes are quite hardy and easy to maintain.

A few tips for growing luscious tomatoes:

- Take the time to fertilize your soil well, using two to three pounds of fertilizer per hundred square feet.

- Whether you buy tomato plants from the store or start them from seed, plant only the strongest and best tomato plants. Look for the ones that are as wide as they are tall. When starting from seed, look for heirloom, organic, and/or open-pollinated seeds.

- When using store bought plants, harden them off (leaving them outdoors in a cool, shady spot and bringing them indoors at night) to acclimate them to the outside temperatures.

- Transplant on a cool, cloudy morning. Position plants so the lowest set of leaves are at soil level. Another strategy is to strip all of the leaves except the top ones and bury the stems horizontally in a shallow trench so that only the top leaves show.

- Leave minimally two feet between seedlings when planting, if you're planning to stake and keep them pruned, so that at maturity, they still get good air circulation.

- Plant only in a location that receives full sun... that means six hours of direct sunlight a day. Also, tomatoes need some protection from wind.

- Pinch off the top of the plant once it has four flower shoots (you can also do the same with lateral shoots) in order to produce more and larger fruits.

- Tomatoes need support in order to keep the fruit away from the ground and from insects. Install strong wire sticks or cages when the plant is very young.

- In order to promote growth, fertilize on a regular basis.

- Watering: Keep the soil moist around the roots in order to prevent the tomatoes from wilting. The best time to water is early morning so that the plant has time to let the water soak in before the hot sun evaporates it. Failure to water your tomatoes on a consistent basis can result in split skins.

Sharing

*"The man who has planted a garden
feels that he has done something for
the good of the world."*

—Charles Dudley Warner

I am always amazed at the power of gardens to transform people (it's the same with babies; they can melt even the toughest exteriors). I've seen people become awestruck in my garden, and it's usually the ones I would least expect to have an emotional reaction. I remember one gentleman in particular, a portly man in his early seventies, who came on a group tour of my garden with his wife. He clearly did not want to be there, and made sure everyone around him knew it. He harrumphed his way from one side of the garden to the other, then suddenly stopped next to the twig-and-vine hut I had up at the time.

"Hey, Marjorie," he bellowed to his wife. "Come take a look-see at this!"

Turns out that he and his brother had built a fort that looked very much like this structure when they were kids. Suddenly, this begrudging man was excitedly telling the whole group about how they had cut down dead branches from the woods behind their house with forbidden Swiss Army knives and worked on their fort in secret for the better part of a year. It was wonderful to watch his entire being come alive as he told the tale inspired by this simple and primitive little structure in my garden. He stopped harrumphing and actually left there smiling.

If I kept my garden all precious and locked up, I wouldn't be making contributions like these to the greater whole of humankind. Yes, it was a sweet and simple little experience, but who knows who Marjorie's husband came into contact with later that day, or what effect his elevated mood had on the people around him.

Those of us who are living creative lives implicitly understand that our lives are made richer because of it. It means something to us to mentor others and share this little bit of understanding and joy we have found so we can pass it along. In this way, we contribute to others, lighting one small spark of creativity at a time until the whole world is illuminated. This isn't about proselytizing; it's about sharing our creations so others can get even the smallest taste of their own inspiration and aspiration.

Sharing is more than just a good karmic virtue that benefits others. Through sharing our creative products, we grow as well. For most of my life, I was very shy about my art forms. I can remember as a child playing classical pieces on the piano, nearing a sense of ecstasy. But if my mother called in from the kitchen to say, "That sounds wonderful, Frannie," I would immediately close up, the spell broken. It felt too private to have it out there for anyone else to see or hear. Years later, even after I spent so much time designing and working in my garden, I was timid and scared. It was again a highly private affair, and disclosing it meant risking vulnerability and potential ridicule. At some point, someone asked to include my garden on a tour. At first I hesitated; why would I want to expose myself this way? But one thing I know about myself is that when I feel afraid, I'm usually facing the next frontier of my growth. I take the fear as a signal that this is the next thing for me to work on. So I said *yes*, with much trepidation.

The first time a tour arrived, I swear I hid in the kitchen as about fifty people pulled up and traipsed through what had been up until then my private world. They touched the trees I'd planted and wandered up and around the stone walls that took so much time and vision to build. After a while, I noticed that a lot of them looked like they were enjoying themselves, so I stepped outside and started talking to a few, bit by bit. I showed them the portfolio of the garden as it was being constructed, and at some point I realized that I felt completely relaxed and at ease. I wasn't pretending to know more than I did, or posturing in any way. This was me, this was my creation, and talking about it felt as natural as breathing.

As more tours came through, my confidence grew. I began to experiment more, and take more risks. Could they just have easily come to my garden that first time and said, "Yuck, why are we here?" Of course! I don't know what would have happened if they hadn't liked it, but I like to think I would have grown from that, too, in some way. Since then, I have shared my garden with thousands of enthusiasts. I love that I may have opened up possibilities for others, the way that a picture of a Gertrude Jekyll garden with retaining walls inspired me to create something similar in my sloped yard all those years ago.

When we share, we give away a little piece of ourselves. We don't lose anything in this giving. In fact, we gain more—more space inside, more room in our hearts, more ease in our interactions. Generosity is boundless, and often infectious. It's like love. A neighbor of mine named Debby has a very special relationship with her grandson Daniel, whose mommy is expecting a new baby any day now. While riding in the car one morning, Daniel turned to Debby and instructed her that she was only allowed to love the new baby *this much* (picture a five year-old holding his thumb and forefinger one inch apart).

Debby hid a smile as she explained to Daniel that he was her first grandchild, and that he would always be very special to her. She assured him she wasn't going to give any of the love she had for him to the new baby—she was simply going to make more.

Daniel's eyes got very wide and, amazed, he asked, "You can do that? You can just make more?"

"You bet I can!" Debby said. "We can always make more. That is the special secret about love."

This is also the special secret about creativity. It's a form of energy, and it follows the natural physical law that energy begets energy. You're not giving your ideas or creative products away so much as making room for new ones to arise. By keeping the energy in motion, your imagining and envisioning powers stay fresh and active, and your capacity to see more possibilities increases.

To share the products of your authentic creation is to pass along your legacy. This is how a piece of us lives on, long after our time here has expired. Our creations don't necessarily make us immortal, but they enable us to leave behind a footprint: a symbol that *I was here.*

For me, I especially love to know that my garden lives on in the memories of the people who are near and dear to me. I was overwhelmed when my close friend Helaine's daughter Jenny asked if she could have her bridal shower in my garden. It was so incredible to grasp that a place I created meant something personal to her and that it would hold a place in her future memory. I treasure knowing that my garden brings loved ones together in love and celebration—and what better purpose could any creative endeavor possibly serve than that?

If you want to bring prosperity to someone in your life, give them a *Lunaria annua* plant, otherwise known as the "money plant." Gardening lore has it that placing one of these in your home is sure to attract wealth and abundance.

Completing

Cycling through the Season

Everything in life has its cycles, many of which are spoken of metaphorically in gardening terms. We say we are *planting a seed* at inception, let things *take root*, console ourselves with the knowledge that *everything has its season.* Was there ever a more exact or profound manifestation of birth and death, beginning and ending, seeds, sprouts, and demise than in the garden?

The end of the gardening season can feel very sad, indeed. The first frost is so devastating! Every single time, though I know it is coming, I feel a loss. A sense of melancholy comes over me and my garden as the late-autumn days get shorter and the air grows colder. But I comfort myself by going through the familiar rituals of putting the garden to bed: cutting away the dead annuals, lifting any of the remaining tubers, cleaning up the debris, bringing in the tropical plants that won't survive outside, and turning the soil for next spring. When I'm all finished and the garden is quiet and barren, it's hard not to feel a little let down. But very soon after, I spend some time looking around at the bare bones and start dreaming all over again.

I think one of the most poignant parts of any creative process is the time it comes to its natural conclusion. It doesn't matter whether you're waving good-bye to your children as they go off on their own, crocheting the last stitch of a blanket, or closing the file on an engaging legal case you put your heart and soul into drafting and arguing—the feeling is always the same: part proud, part sad, part satisfied, and always bittersweet. It's time to let go of this particular cycle, dust yourself off, and look within to see what's next for you.

In this last stage of unearthing your creative roots, you will examine why it is so essential to celebrate the completion of any creative cycle, and what it means, as a gardener and a creative spirit, to come back to the beginning—just you, your space, your breath, your soul—to rejuvenate and renew once again.

Celebrating

"But he who kisses the Joy as it flies,
lives in eternity's sunrise."

—William Blake

To celebrate means to mark an occasion or moment in time in some significant way. We traditionally think of celebrating as having a party for a birthday or toasting to our anniversaries, good news, or accomplishments. But it is also important as creative beings that we celebrate when our endeavors come to their own natural fruition or conclusion. For the same reason that we celebrate life milestones, we need to step back for a moment and note all we have done, honoring the journey for simply having happened.

I know a pair of women in their thirties who run their own architectural firm. They put a lot of time and work into their designs, and they make sure they celebrate each and every job when it is completed. The day the last detail goes in on one of their projects, they do something together to mark it. Sometimes they bring along their spouses and have a celebratory dinner, or sometimes they take an hour or two out of their day and go to a spa for a little pampering. The celebrations aren't big, but after all the work they put in, these dinners and massages certainly are sweet. I think this is a lovely ritual, because it enables them to jump off the treadmill of working even for a short while and honor their accomplishments.

Our moments do not have to be big, major accomplishments to merit celebration. I celebrated everything with my kids, including when Erika learned to roller-skate and when Jason earned a B+ on a paper he'd worked hard on. In the grand scheme of things, these may not have seemed like major accomplishments, but that wasn't what we were celebrating in the first place. We were celebrating their courage, their tenacity, and their willingness to show up with all they had in whatever they did—not unlike every single one of us in our creative endeavors.

The garden is always a work in progress, and unlike finite creations such as a building, it's never really done. It does, however, come to a natural conclusion each year when the weather turns chilly and the bloom fades. There is a letting-go process that needs to happen whenever we complete a cycle. For finite creations, like buildings, this happens when they're declared finished. For cyclical ones, like gardening, or relating to others, this happens when one particular season comes to an end. Through celebrating, we can honor and let go of *what was* to once again embrace the present reality of *what is* so we can move on into *what will* be.

Since the dawn of time, humankind has worked and lived in accordance with the seasons. In today's world where we air-condition our summers and heat our winters, it can be easy to fall out of step with the organic rhythm of the natural world, but with even the tiniest bit of consciousness we can immediately reconnect with the greater force in play all around us. Throughout the ages, late autumn has been a time of harvest. The season has always been a quieter kind of celebration—a more reflective, internal kind in which we acknowledge the land and give thanks for the bounty and beauty it provides. To celebrate the harvest at the end of the planting season realigns us with the pattern of nature, bringing us back to our own naturalness. We are particles in nature, after all. We are intrinsically part of the cycle—no more, and no less.

This year, at the end of the season, I think I am going to cook a big dinner for all the people I love most in the world. I'll make a wonderful salad using the last of my fat, ripe tomatoes. I'll dry whatever flowers are left to make a welcoming wreath for the front door, and bring in some stalks of the dried grasses and put them in tall vases in the center of the table. I'll take some cuttings from the plants I bring inside and give one to each of my guests, so these plants will live on in dozens of small reincarnations in their homes. It's been a long, fruitful season, with some great breakthroughs and some tough challenges, and it's time to celebrate it for all it was—and to celebrate the growth I experienced as a result.

 To try

Find a way that is meaningful for you to celebrate the end of the season in your garden (even if you live in a warm climate—the seasonal changes there are more subtle, but they are still there). You can have a gathering like the one I'm planning, or perhaps have a harvest party where everyone comes to the garden to actually help clean up and put the garden to bed for the winter. They can help cut down any flowers and snip off any veggies that are left outside, and each person who participates gets a basket of these goodies to take home.

Or, of course, you could simply celebrate the natural end of the cycle in sweet and blissful solitude.

PUTTING THE GARDEN TO BED

- ✤ Make sure that all beds are weed-free and mulched.

- ✤ Pull out all dead annuals.

- ✤ Take in non-hardy plants before the frost comes and use as houseplants.

- ✤ Dig up tubers (like dahlias and cannas) in climates where they're not hardy and store indoors for the winter.

- ✤ Cut back all perennials that you don't want to leave standing over the winter.

- ✤ Bring in all furniture and containers that you don't want kept outside in the cold.

> *"The earth laughs in flowers."*
> *—Ralph Waldo Emerson*

Renewing

"Though an old man,
I am but a young gardener."
—Thomas Jefferson

One my favorite things about the culture of gardeners is our belief in eternal growth. As stewards of this land, we know that even as we are putting our gardens to bed, life will bloom again in the spring. Come what may, we'll be back here again before long, shaking the sleep of winter off these magical places and bringing it to life once again. This is so basic, yet so very profound.

FORCING BRANCHES FROM
FLOWERING TREES

Often just the sight of new buds beginning to appear on flowering trees is enough to rouse us from the doldrums of winter. As soon as I see the buds of cherry blossoms, or forsythia, or magnolia, I know spring can't be far behind.

Here are some tips for forcing branches from flowering trees so that you can bring them indoors to enjoy:

- Forcing should be done in late winter or spring, depending on where you live, when the buds of flowering bushes and trees are still closed tight.

- Make sharp diagonal cuts on the branches.

- Remove leaves and buds from the bottom eight inches.

- Place the branches in a bucket half full of tepid water.

- Store in a cool place, away from the sun.

- Change the water every other day.

- Once buds start blooming, place your spring-flowering branches in a beautiful vase in a location where they can be noticed and enjoyed.

In any creative process, renewal happens after we clear the slate. Like our garden, we need to take some time to rest and reflect on all we have done, to rejuvenate our minds and our spirits. As sad as the end of the season is, and as much as I love the work of gardening, my mind and body are usually tired by this point, and I relish the down time of winter to regenerate myself. Throughout the cold months, as I inwardly reflect on what I did this past year and what I might dream about for next, I think of my bulbs, snug and secure under the cold earth, actively resting, too, so they can awaken into their magnificence come springtime.

Creative renewal is always possible. There is always another dream to put into vision, another innovation to plan, more choices to make, more risks to take, and more work and play to enjoy. The spirit of creativity, once awakened within us, shows up in everything we do, again and again. Like our gardens, our creative natures thrive on the constant cycle of pursuit and rest, action and reflection.

We could talk forever about the miracle of the seasons, or of how we have grown and changed, or what we might do next year. Marjorie Fish once said, "I could go on and on. But that's just what gardening is—going on and on."

I couldn't agree more.

Further Reading

Ackerman, Diane. *A Natural History of the Senses* (Vintage Books Edition, 1995).

Ausubel, Kenny. *Restoring the Earth: Visionary Solutions from the Bioneers* (H.J. Kramer, 1997).

Artemis, Angela. *The Intuition Principle: How to Attract the Life You Dream Of* (Synchronicity Publishing, 2011).

Baldwin, Debra Lee. *Designing with Succulents* (Timber Press, 2007).

Baldwin, Debra Lee. *Succulent Container Gardens: Design Eye-Catching Displays with 350 Plants* (Timber Press, 2009).

Beckwith, Michael Bernard. *Life Visioning: A Transformative Process for Activating Your Unique Gifts and Highest Potential* (Sounds True, 2012).

Beckwith, Michael Bernard. *The Answer is You: Heart Sets and Mind Sets for Self-Discovery* (Agape Media, 2009).

Benyus, Janine. *Biomimicry: Innovation Inspired by Nature* (Harper Collins, 2002).

Brown, Brené. *The Gifts of Imperfection: Let Go of Who You Think You're Supposed to Be and Embrace Who You Are* (Hazelden, 2010).

Brown, Stuart. *Play: How it Shapes the Brain, Opens the Imagination, and Invigorates the Soul* (Penguin Group, 2009).

Buzzell, Linda and Craig Chalquist. *Ecotherapy: Healing with Nature in Mind* (Sierra Club Books, 2009).

Campbell, Joseph. *The Power of Myth* (Anchor Books, 1988).

Capek, Karl. *The Gardener's Year* (Modern Library, 2002).

Carson, Rachel. *Silent Spring* (First Mariner Books Edition, 2002).

Chopra, Deepak. *The Seven Spiritual Laws of Success* (Amber-Allen Publishing and New World Publishing, 1993).

Cornell, Joseph. *The Sky and Earth Touched Me* (Crystal Clarity Publishers, 2014).

Csikszentmihalyi, Mihaly. *Flow: The Psychology of Optimal Experience* (Harper and Row, 1990).

Csikszentmihalyi, Mihaly. *Creativity: The Psychology of Discovery and Invention* (Harper Perennial Modern Classics, 2013).

Darke, Rick. *The American Woodland Garden* (Timber Press, 2002).

Das, Lama Surya. *Buddha Standard Time: Awakening to the Infinite Possibilities of Now* (HarperOne, 2011).

Das, Lama Surya. *Awakening the Buddhist Heart: Integrating Love, Meaning, and Connection into Every Part of Your Life* (Broadway, 2000).

Dossey, Larry. *One Mind: How Our Individual Mind Is Part of a Greater Consciousness and Why It Matters* (Hay House, 2013).

Dossey, Larry. *The Extraordinary Healing Power of Ordinary Things* (Three Rivers Press, 2006).

Eisenstein, Charles. *The More Beautiful World Our Hearts Know Is Possible* (North Atlantic Books, 2013).

Estabrook, Barry. *Tomatoland: How Modern Industrial Agriculture Destroyed Our Most Alluring Fruit* (Andrews McNeil Publishing, 2012).

Finley, Guy. *The Secret of Letting Go* (Llewellyn Worldwide, 2007).

Finley, Guy. *The Courage to Be Free: Discover Your Original Fearless Self* (Red Wheel/Weiser, 2007).

Gardner, Howard. *Frames of Mind: Theories of Multiple Intelligence* (Basic Books, 2011).

Gatto, John Taylor. *Dumbing Us Down: The Hidden Curriculum of Compulsory Schooling* (New Society Publishers, 2005).

Gawain, Shakti. *Creative Visualization: Use the Power of Your Imagination to Create What You Want in Your Life* (New World Library, 2002).

Goddard, Neville. *The Power of Awareness* (Pacific Publishing Studio, 2010).

Goldberg, Natalie. *Writing Down The Bones: Freeing The Writer Within, 2nd Edition* (Shambala Publications, 2005).

Goldberger, Miriam. *Taming Wildflowers: Bringing the Beauty and Splendor of Nature's Blooms Into Your Own Backyard* (St. Lynn's Press, 2013).

Greenlee, John and Saxon Holt. *The American Meadow Garden* (Timber Press, 2009).

Hanh, Thich Nhat. *The Energy of Prayer: How To Deepen Your Spiritual Practice* (Parallax Press, 2006).

Hawken, Paul. *Blessed Unrest: How the Largest Social Movement in History Is Restoring Grace, Justice, and Beauty to the World* (Penguin Books, 2007).

Holden, Robert. *Happiness Now: Timeless Wisdom for Feeling Good Fast* (Hay House, 2007).

Holden, Robert. *Follow Your Joy: 6 Creative Principles for Living a Happier Life*—CD (Hay House, 2011).

Johnsen, Jan. *Heaven is a Garden: Designing Serene Spaces for Inspiration and Reflection* (St. Lynn's Press, 2014).

Johnson, Trebbe. *The World Is a Waiting Lover: Desire and the Quest for the Beloved* (New World Library, 2005).

Jung, Carl. *Modern Man in Search of a Soul* (Harcourt, Inc., 1933).

Jung, Carl. *The Undiscovered Self,* Reprint Edition (New American Library, 2006).

Kabat-Zinn, Jon. *Wherever You Go, There You Are* (Hyperion, 1994).

Kingsbury, Noel. *Gardening with Perennials: Lessons from Chicago's Lurie Garden* (Timber Press, 2014).

Kingsbury, Noel and Piet Oudolf. *Planting: A New Perspective* (Timber Press, 2013).

Kleon, Austin. *Steal Like An Artist: 10 Things Nobody Told You About Being Creative* (Workman Publishing, 2012).

Levertov, Denise. *The Life Around Us: Selected Poems On Nature* (New Directions Books, 1997).

Lord, Tony. *Gardening at Sissinghurst* (Frances Lincoln Ltd, 1995).

Louv, Richard. *Last Child in the Woods: Saving Our Children From Nature Deficit Dis-Order* (Algonquin Books, 2008).

Maslow, Abraham. *Religions, Values, and Peak Experiences* (Penguin Books, 1976).

Maslow, Abraham. *The Farther Reaches of Human Nature* (Penguin Books, 1976).

May, Rollo. *The Courage to Create* (W.W. Norton & Co., 1994).

Merton, Thomas. *New Seeds of Contemplation* (New Directions Book, 2007).

Miller, Karen Maezen, *Paradise in Plain Sight: Lessons from a Zen Garden* (New World Library, 2014).

Morrison, Susan, and Rebecca Sweet. *Garden Up! Smart Vertical Gardening for Small and Large Spaces* (Cool Springs Press, 2011).

Murray, Elizabeth. *Living Life in Full Bloom: 120 Daily Practices to Deepen Your Passion, Creativity & Relationships* (Rodale, 2014).

Murray, Elizabeth. *Monet's Passion* (Pomegrante Communications, 2010).

Nachmanovitch, Stephen. *Free Play: The Power of Improvisation In Life and Art* (Penguin Group, 1990).

Nash, Dee. *The 20-30 Something Garden Guide: A No-Fuss, Down and Dirty, Gardening 101 for Anyone Who Wants to Grow Stuff* (St. Lynns Press, 2014).

Oliver, Mary. *The Leaf and The Cloud* (Da Capo Press, 2000).

Ondra, Nancy and Saxon Holt. *Grasses: Versatile Partners for Uncommon Design* (Storey Publishing, 2002).

Oudolf, Piet and Henk Gerritsen. *Planting the Natural Garden* (Timber Press, 2003).

Oudolf, Piet and Noel Kingsbury. *Designing with Plants* (Timber Press, 1999).

Pavord, Anna. *Hidcote Manor Garden: Gloucestershire* (National Trust Guidebooks, 1993).

Penick, Pam. *Lawn Gone!: Low-Maintenance, Sustainable, Attractive Alternatives For Yard* (Ten Speed Press, 2013).

Plotkin, Bill. *Nature and the Human Soul* (New World Library, 2008).

Pollan, Michael. *The Botany of Desire: A Plant's Eye View of the World* (Random House, 2001).

Pressfield, Steven. *The War of Art: Winning the Inner Creative Battle* (Rugged Land, 2002).

Prinzing, Debra. *Slow Flowers: Four Seasons of Locally Grown Bouquets from the Garden, Meadow and Farm* (St. Lynn's Press, 2013).

Prinzing, Debra and David Perry. *The 50 Mile Bouquet: Seasonal, Local and Sustainable Flowers* (St. Lynn's Press, 2012).

Ram Dass with Rameshwar Das. *Be Love Now: The Path of the Heart* (Harper Collins, 2010).

Roach, Margaret. *The Backyard Parable: The Lessons on Gardening, and Life* (Hachette Book Group, 2013).

Rohr, Richard. *Eager to Love: The Alternative Way of Francis of Assisi* (Franciscan Media, 2014).

Rohr, Richard. *Immortal Diamond: The Search for Our True Self* (Jossey-Bass, 2013).

Ruiz, Don Miguel. *The Four Agreements: A Practical Guide to Personal Happiness* (Amber-Allen Publishing, 2012).

Shapiro, Rami. *Recovery—The Sacred Act: The Twelve Steps as Spiritual Practice* (Skylights Path Publishing, 2009).

Shapiro, Rami. *Perennial Wisdom for the Spiritually Independent: Sacred Teachings—Annotated and Explained* (Skylights Path Publishing, 2013).

Shimoff, Marci, with Carol Kline. *Happy for No Reason: 7 Steps to Being Happy from the Inside Out* (Free Press, 2008).

Shimoff, Marci, with Carol Kline. *Love for No Reason: 7 Steps to Creating a Life of Unconditional Love* (Free Press, 2010).

Smith, Edward. *The Vegetable Gardener's Bible* (Storey Publishing, 2009).

Stewart, Amy. Wicked Plants: *The Weed That Killed Lincoln's Mother & Other Botanical Atrocities* (Algonquin Books, 2009).

Stewart, Amy. *The Drunken Botanist: The Plants That Create the World's Great Drinks* (Algonquin Books, 2013).

Sweet, Rebecca. *Refresh Your Garden Design with Color, Texture & Form* (Horticulture Books, 2013).

Tallamy, Doug and Rick Darke. *Bringing Nature Home: How You Can Sustain Wildlife with Native Plants, Updated and Expanded* (Timber Press, 2009).

Tharp, Twyla. *The Creative Habit: Learn It and Use It for Life* (Simon & Schuster, 2003).

Thoreau, Henry David. *Walden* (Dover Publications, 1995).

Tompkins, Peter, and Christopher Bird. *The Secret Life of Plants: A Fascinating Account of the Physical, Emotional, and Spiritual Relations Between Plants* (First Perennial Library Edition, 1989).

Tsu, Lao and Jane English. *Tao Te Ching—25th Anniversary Edition* (Vintage Books, 1997).

Tolle, Eckhart. *A New Earth: Awakening to Your Life's Purpose* (Penguin Group, 2005).

Walliser, Jessica. *Attracting Beneficial Bugs to Your Garden: A Natural Approach to Pest Control* (Timber Press, 2014).

Weil, Andrew. *Spontaneous Happiness: A New Path to Emotional Well-Being* (Little, Brown & Company, 2011).

Weil, Andrew. *Spontaneous Healing: How to Discover and Enhance Your Body's Natural Ability to Maintain and Heal Itself* (Knopf, 1995).

Wilson, Edward. *On Human Nature* (Harvard University Press, 1994).

Yoest, Helen. *Plants with Benefits: An Uninhibited Guide to the Aphrodisiac Herbs, Fruits, Flowers & Veggies in Your Garden* (St. Lynn's Press, 2014).

Gardening Resources

Here are some of my favorite online sources for plant material, gardening tools, and other gardening supplies, which I've personally used over the years. It's not meant to be an exhaustive list of gardening resources.

A.M. Leonard's Gardener's Edge
www.gardenersedge.com
An excellent source for composting, fertilizers, pest control, plant support, raised beds, tools, watering and irrigation, weather, yard and landscape, and much more. I'm a big fan of their Leonard Deluxe Stainless Steel Soil Knife.

Authentic Haven Brand Natural Brew Soil Conditioner Tea
www.ahavenbrand.com
Haven's Natural Brew Tea conditions the soil so your plant's root system can better absorb the nutrients needed to build a strong, healthy root base.

Baker Creek Heirloom Seeds
www.rareseeds.com
Founded by Jere Gettle in 1998, this family-owned and operated company has grown to offer 1600 varieties of vegetable, flower, and herb seeds from over 75 countries—the largest selection of rare,

heirloom varieties in the United States. All of their seeds are non-hybrid, non-GMO, non-treated, and non-patented. They're one of my go-to sources for seeds. Exciting new varieties are offered each year that will whet your appetite and inspire you to experiment.

Brent and Becky's Bulbs

www.brentandbeckysbulbs.com

Brent and Becky Heath are hybridizers of daffodils and third-generation bulb growers. They test many unusual and specialty bulbs on their 28-acre farm and garden. A fantastic selection of fall and summer bulbs that are high quality and fairly priced.

Colorblends

www.colorblends.com

A third-generation wholesale flower merchant with strong relationships to tulip bulb growers in the Netherlands who sell to home gardeners as well as wholesalers. Their product is excellent and prices are competitive.

DeWit Garden Tools

www.dewit.co

A family run business of high quality gardening tools, hand-forged in Holland. For sturdy tools that will grow old with you, these are worth checking out.

Digging Dog Nursery

www.diggingdog.com

A family operated retail and mail order plant nursery specializing in unusual and hard to find perennials, ornamental grasses, shrubs, trees, and vines.

Gardener's Supply

www.gardeners.com

The go-to source for anything having to do with organic pest control and garden accessories for vegetable, flower, and elevated gardening, raised beds, tools, watering, arbors, and much more.

Gossler Farms Nursery

www.gosslerfarms.com

Owned and operated by Marj Gossler and her two sons, Roger and Eric, the nursery is situated on 10 acres in Willamette, Oregon. They have an excellent selection of woody bushes, trees, and evergreens. Unusual varieties like Davidia involucrata can be found here, along with a large variety of hydrangeas and magnolias.

Greer Gardens

www.greergardens.com

Owned by Harold and Nancy Greer, Greer Gardens (near Eugene, Oregon) offers more than 4,500 varieties of perennials, trees, and shrubs. It's gained a reputation for the rare and unusual plants ordered (online or by phone) by people across the country and throughout the world.

Heirloom Roses

www.heirloomroses.com

When I initially became interested in old-fashioned roses, I scoured their beautiful catalog, learned about the different varieties, and bought several bushes from them over the years.

High Country Gardens

www.highcountrygardens.com

David Salman, the owner of High Country Gardens, is a pioneer in sustainability. His nursery offers plants, products, and information that supports long-term ecological balance. High Country offers a fantastic selection of xeric plants and is at the top of my list for unusual and exciting varieties of agastache and salvia. Over the years, I've bought unusual native and xeric specimens from David that I'd be hard pressed to find elsewhere.

Kurt Bluemel, Inc.—wholesale
www.kurtbluemel.com
Kurt Bluemel (who died a few years ago) is acknowledged as one of the founding fathers of the ornamental grass movement. His wholesale nursery, which was founded in 1964, offers a wonderful selection of ornamental grasses, bamboo, perennials, ferns, sedges, rushes, and other exotic nursery plant material. I bought hundreds of plants from him throughout the years.

Renee's Garden
www.reneesgarden.com
Renee's Garden is operated by Renee Shepherd, who has decades of experience in the business. All of the heirloom and gourmet vegetable, flower, and herb seeds in the catalog are Renee's personal selections, chosen for excellence in flavor, color, ease of growing, and garden performance for home gardeners. Each season when I peruse through Renee's catalog to see what new varieties she's offering, I feel her caring attitude and artistic personality come through the pages.

The Antique Rose Emporium
www.antiqueroseemporium.com
A wonderful resource for antique roses. It became my source for hybrid musk climbing roses that can thrive in partial shade. Two of my favorites are Lavender Lassie and Cecile Brunner, which also have the added bonus of being repeat bloomers. Excellent quality and fair prices.

Fran Sorin is an author, gardening and creativity expert, coach, and speaker. For over a decade, she has been the gardening correspondent for CBS radio news, where her Digging Deep gardening features are broadcast several times a week throughout the United States.

She spent years as a gardening authority on Philadelphia's Fox and NBC stations, was the regular gardening contributor on NBC's *Weekend Today Show,* and made several appearances on CNN, MSNBC, Lifetime, HGTV, DIY, and the Discovery Channel. She has been a celebrity spokesperson for ourhouse.com, MSNBC, and Garden Weasel. In addition, she has written dozens of articles about gardening and well-being for *USA Weekend Magazine, Radius Magazine,* and iVillage.

Fran is also one of the co-founders of, and has written hundreds of articles for, www.GardeningGoneWild.com, an award-winning blog—with a roster of renowned gardening authors, designers, photographers, broadcasters, and teachers. She is a graduate of the University of Chicago with honors in psychology and One Spirit

Interfaith Seminary in New York City, where she was ordained as an interfaith minister.

Through her coaching practice, Fran helps clients open to possibilities and dream big—bigger than they ever thought possible. Then she helps them discover new ways of creating their dreams and living a life filled with joy, well-being, and abundance.

Fran's website is filled with free resources that will inspire and galvanize you to improve your life. When you sign up for Fran's newsletter, you will be the first to know about any new courses, workshops, or books and will be offered exclusive discounts. To meet Fran and learn more, visit www.FranSorin.com.